WELSH HISTORY MAKERS

By the same author:

Goodbye To Morning, a biography of Mary Webb
Shrewsbury and Shropshire
Shropshire History Makers

WELSH
HISTORY MAKERS

Dorothy P. H. Wrenn

EP PUBLISHING LIMITED

This edition first published 1976 by EP Publishing Limited
East Ardsley, Wakefield, Yorkshire, England

ISBN 0 7158 1193 2

The author and publisher gratefully acknowledge the following for kindly supplying
photographs:

Mr. Don Griffiths, *County Times & Express*,
Newtown (page 70); the National Library of
Wales (7, 9, 12, 14, 20, 21, 24, 35, 37, 50, 52,
54, 57, 58, 65); the National Portrait
Gallery (26, 29, 31, 39, 59); Radio Times
Hulton Picture Library (42, 43, 46, 49, 69,
73, 74, 75, 79, 81, 83, 86, 87, 89, 90, 94, 96);
the Victoria and Albert Museum (28, 62, 63,
64).

Text set in 11/12 pt. Monotype Baskerville, printed by photolithography,
and bound in Great Britain by Robert MacLehose and Co. Ltd.,
Printers to the University of Glasgow

Preface

As an alien from the English side of Offa's Dyke, I must apologise for trespassing on territory which is not mine, though the Border has always been debatable ground. I have tried in my accounts to convey the essential 'Welshness' of every character, which appears to me to have had in every case a bearing upon the person's life. For there is a Celtic mystique, which has been consistent through the centuries. Owain Glyndwr, Robert Owen and Aneurin Bevan all championed the cause of the inarticulate oppressed. Both Giraldus Cambrensis and Dylan Thomas wrote in loving detail of their native land. Llywelyn Fawr, driving the English out of Wales, was demanding the very things which members of Plaid Cymru seek today. And where could one find a face more typically Welsh than Hester Lynch Salusbury's?

My thanks are due to my many Welsh friends who have given me help and advice while compiling this book. In particular, I would like to thank the National Library of Wales, Miss Dora Thomas and Mr. and Mrs. W. F. Jones for their invaluable assistance in obtaining illustrations, and Mrs. Olwen Purslow for kindly supplying so many sources of information.

Dorothy P. H. Wrenn

Contents

Giraldus Cambrensis, *c.* 1146–1222

Giraldus Cambrensis, 'Gerald of Wales'
from his tomb in St. David's Cathedral

During the century which followed the conquest of England, the authority of the Norman and Angevin kings over Wales was constantly in dispute. The Marcher lords, whose castles had been built in the borderland between England and Wales in order to deter Welsh raiders from invading the lands granted to them by the Conqueror, had gradually annexed more territory on the Welsh side of their boundaries, but here their rule was constantly disputed. In South Wales, the hold of the Norman-French barons was stronger—it was in the interest of various kings to support them, for the Carmarthen area provided a strategic starting-point for attacks upon Ireland. But in North and Central Wales, both people and princes clung stubbornly to their own language, laws and customs, defying the jurisdiction of the Anglo-Norman rulers. And so mountainous was the terrain that, away from the March, these Welsh princes were on the whole left alone. Campaigning in the mountains frequently proved to be wasteful of men, money and supplies, and the internecine feuds of the Welsh prevented any of their princes from gaining so much power as to become a genuine threat to England.

One of these Welsh princes was Rhys ap Tewdyr, Lord of Deheubarth. Rhys had a daughter, the princess Nest, who was so beautiful that she became known as 'The Helen of Wales'. Like the original Helen, Nest was at one time the cause of strife, for Owain of Powys kidnapped her from her father's castle of Cardigan. He wanted to marry her, but Rhys had other ambitions for his daughter. Owain was forced to give her up, and her father arranged that she should marry a Norman, Gerald de Windsor, Lord of Pembroke Castle. One of their daughters, Angharad, married another Norman, William de Barri, Lord of Manorbier and of the island of Barri (Barry Island). They were the parents of Giraldus Cambrensis.

Giraldus Cambrensis is the Latin for 'Gerald of Wales'—not, as is often stated, 'Gerald the Welshman'. Gerald had more Norman blood in his veins than Welsh; he received a fairly cosmopolitan education, and he understood Welsh, but he was not a fluent speaker of the language. He developed, however, a fierce passion for the land of his birth, and longed to see the country independent of any attempt at control by the Anglo-Normans. He retained a lifelong affection for his birthplace, Manorbier, as a description which he included in his *Itinerary Through Wales* shows:

> The castle is called Maenor Pyrr. . . . It is excellently well defended by turrets and bulwarks . . . having on the northern and southern sides a fine fish-pond under its walls, as conspicuous for its grand appearance as for the depth of its waters; and a beautiful orchard on the same side, inclosed on one part by a vineyard and on the other by a wood remarkable for the height of its hazel trees. . . . Towards the west the Severn Sea, bending its course to Ireland, enters a shallow bay at some distance from the castle. This country . . . is the most beautiful, as well as the most powerful, district of Wales . . . and the place I have just described, the most delightful part of it. It is evident, therefore, that Maenor Pyrr is the pleasantest spot in Wales.

As the son of a Norman nobleman, Gerald de Barri would have had every opportunity to become a knight. But he had no warlike ambitions. He relates how, as a child, he would construct churches and monasteries of sand on the shore, although his brothers built castles. He loved learning,

and developed a considerable interest in visiting neighbouring churches and abbeys. His family called him 'the little bishop', but his curiosity was due less to religious fervour than to the fact that, in most abbeys, he had access to learned clerics and to books. Scholarship was, at that time, in the hands of the church; the layman was assumed to devote his talents to work and to warfare. So it was decided that Gerald should take Holy Orders.

David Fitzgerald, one of Gerald's uncles, was Bishop of St. David's, the supreme cathedral of Wales. To him Gerald was sent to be educated as a clerk. From the first, he showed a remarkable aptitude and took an interest not only in Divinity but in everything that came his way. His interests included Geography, History, Ethics, Law, Biography, Natural History and Poetry. He continued his studies at the Abbey of St. Peter, in Gloucester, from where he proceeded to the University of Paris. There was, of course, a great deal of coming and going between England and France at that time, for the rulers of England still considered themselves in all essentials to be French. Universities had not the settled character to which we are accustomed; students travelled to hear any teacher whom they considered worth following. This was made easy by the fact that Latin was the universal language of the educated man, and the vast majority of educated men were connected in some way or other with the church.

Gerald enjoyed his three years at Paris, and in addition to pursuing his studies he took a lively interest in life in the French capital, making notes on events of importance. One night in August 1165, he was awakened by the pealing of all the bells of the city, and the flickering glow of flames. He rushed to his window, thinking that Paris was on fire. The narrow ways were thronged with jubilant citizens, and he soon learned that they

Manorbier Castle, birthplace of Gerald and described by him as 'the pleasantest spot in Wales'

had made bonfires in the streets as a sign of rejoicing because the Queen of France had given birth to an heir. 'By the grace of God,' an exultant Frenchman told him, 'there is born to us this night a king who shall be a hammer to the king of the English.'

Gerald, whose studies had done much to sharpen his own intense national pride, also longed to be a hammer to the English, and in subsequent years his opportunity was to come.

In 1170, or thereabouts, he returned to Wales, took Holy Orders and became Archdeacon of Brecon, Prebendary of Hereford and Canon of St. David's. His uncle, the Bishop, was ageing, and his able young nephew was of great practical help to him. Gerald, in his turn, learned a great deal about the administration of the See. St. David's was under the administration of the Archbishop of Canterbury, and Gerald, during the five years in which he acted as his uncle's unofficial secretary and right hand, developed two consuming ambitions. He wanted to succeed David Fitzgerald as Bishop of St. David's, but more than this he wanted to see St. David's recognised as a metropolitan cathedral, so that the church of Wales could be completely free of English domination. He was not alone in his views, and when the Bishop died in 1176 the Chapter nominated the young Archdeacon of Brecon as a candidate for the king's choice as his successor.

The Welsh ecclesiastics, however, had reckoned without the king. Henry II had already successfully fought one battle with the church in his own country, and the victory had cost him dear—the life of his friend, Thomas Beckett. Gerald made no secret of his admiration for Beckett; he visualised himself defying the power of the crown in Wales as Beckett had done in England. Henry also foresaw this same possibility. He wanted no more martyrs, and it was his policy to avoid putting too much power into the hands of any Welsh family. Already he had appointed the Lord Rhys,

Gerald's cousin, as his justiciar in Pembroke. Both Rhys and Gerald were ambitious, competent men and Henry was too wily to give them an opportunity to unite against him.

Peremptorily he summoned the Chapter of St. David's to London, where he compelled them to elect Peter de Leia, the Prior of Wenlock, as their Bishop. De Leia occupied himself with the re-building of St. David's—it was he who was responsible for the cathedral as it stands today. Gerald, bitterly disappointed, relinquished his church offices and returned to Paris, where he continued his studies and, on occasion, taught.

But Henry II had been impressed by the clever young Welshman. In 1183, the Lord Rhys attacked some of the English castles in Pembroke and the king asked Gerald to persuade his kinsman to make peace. As a result of his mediation the rebellion was stopped, and he was rewarded by being appointed a Court Chaplain. His influence in South Wales was obviously considerable and no doubt Henry was not sorry to find an opportunity to utilise his talents and at the same time get him well away from the Lord Rhys. The young Prince John, just eighteen, had been created 'Lord of Ireland'. In 1185 he paid a state visit to Dublin with his entourage, and Gerald accompanied him as his chaplain. Here he remained for two years, during which time he wrote two books about Ireland and the Irish. He also gives an interesting little vignette of the young Prince John, who

. . . being himself young and little more than a boy, followed the counsel of young men whom he took with him, who were utterly unknown in Ireland and themselves knew nothing, whereas he rebuffed the honest and discreet men whom he found there, who knew customs and habits of the country, treating them as though they were foreigners and of little worth.

Gerald's opinion of John was always poor.

In 1187, Saracens, led by Saladin, captured the holy city of Jerusalem and the Christian world united in a movement to rescue from the Infidel the places where Christ had lived. A new Crusade, the third, was proclaimed, and the following year King Henry II sent his chief minister, Ranulf de Glanville, and Baldwin, Archbishop of Canterbury, into Wales to recruit men to fight in the Holy Land. A tour of Wales was planned, and the journey was so arranged that the Archbishop might celebrate Mass in each of the Welsh cathedrals, St. David's, St. Asaph, Llandaff and Bangor. This was not arranged solely in order to encourage as many Welshmen as possible to take the cross; it was also a move to demonstrate the authority of Canterbury over the church in Wales. Gerald, who was a man of high repute and had many Welsh relatives of rank, was appointed to accompany the Archbishop. He was flattered by the distinction conferred upon him, so decided to pocket his pride and forget his ambition to become Bishop of St. David's—for the time being, at least.

The party set out from Radnor in March 1188, and Gerald was the first Welshman to take the cross, for he volunteered to join the Crusade immediately the Archbishop concluded his first sermon, though in the event he never went to Palestine. He wrote a lively account of the journey—*The Itinerary Through Wales*, in which, together with his *Description of Wales*, he gives a detailed account of his native country in the late twelfth and early thirteenth centuries.

The stories he tells of the things seen or heard during the journey are lively, amusing and sometimes very far-fetched. He mentions, for instance, one lake amongst the mountains of Eryri on which there was a floating island, which frequently astonished the local shepherds by carrying their flocks to the opposite shore. Another lake was populated by fish, all of which were one-eyed! But he recounts facts as well, as, for example:

I shall not omit mentioning another event which occurred in our days. Owen, son of Gruffyth, prince of North Wales, had many sons, but only one legitimate, namely Iorwerth Drwyndwn, which in Welsh means 'flat-nosed', who had a son named Llywelyn. This young man, being only twelve years of age, began during the period of our journey to molest his uncles David and Roderic. . . . Within a few years the legitimate son, destitute of lands or money . . . bravely expelled from North Wales those who were born of incest.

'This young man', who asserted his rights at so early an age, became Llywelyn the Great.

Gerald remained in the service of the Crown for another eight years, travelling between England, Wales, Ireland and France. He was in France in 1189 when Henry II died, broken-hearted because his sons had joined the French king in rebellion against him. Gerald had little sympathy for Henry, whom he felt was being justly punished for the murder of Thomas Beckett. Richard I, his successor, obviously well aware of Gerald's influence in Wales, sent him there immediately, with orders to do what he could to prevent the Welsh from attacking the castles in South Wales and on the March. In 1191 or 1192, he once again entered the service of Prince John, who frequently acted as regent during Richard's absence in France or on a Crusade. Gerald was very anxious to make another visit to Ireland, and tried to persuade the prince to return there. But John disliked the Irish, and refused.

In 1198, Peter de Leia died, and Gerald, together with three other candidates, all with Welsh connections, was for a second time nominated for the Bishopric of St. David's. But the Archbishop of Canterbury, zealous for the power of the English church, refused to consider a Welshman. The Chapter of St. David's, offended at this peremptory rejection of all their candidates, united in support of Gerald because they were aware that he felt so strongly about the independence of the church in Wales that he would be prepared to stand up to the Archbishop.

It was decided that a deputation should be sent to King Richard, who was in France, urging him to overrule the Archbishop and to appoint Gerald. But by the time the emissaries reached France, Richard Coeur-de-Lion was dead, killed by an arrow fired during the siege of Chaluz. John was his successor.

John knew Gerald well. He had been attached to him ever since their visit to Ireland, when the new King had been a young man. He was disposed to further Gerald's suit, and in June 1199 agreed verbally that he should be appointed Bishop of St. David's. But meanwhile the Archbishop of Canterbury had elected the Prior of Llantony as Bishop, and had made it clear that he would brook no opposition.

Gerald urged the Chapter to resist this high-handed action. He had two main points to bring forward; first, he hoped that the new King would back him, and secondly, he felt that, if he could be elected, in defiance of the Archbishop, he would be in a position to establish the independence of the Welsh church from the authority of Canterbury. He set out for Rome, in order to consult the Pope about his claim.

The Pope, Innocent III, was a lover of learning and Gerald presented him with six of his books, which Innocent kept by his bedside and encouraged his cardinals to read. But letters from the Archbishop of Canterbury complicated the suit with regard to St. David's. Gerald was rejected because of his family connections in Wales. This caught him in the raw; 'Because I am a Welshman,' he asked the Pope indignantly, 'am I to be debarred from all preferment in Wales?'

He put forward the claims of the See of

St. David's Cathedral, in which Gerald was buried

St. David's to special preferment, basing his arguments on the ancient history of the church in Wales. Pope Innocent was favourably disposed towards his passionate arguments, and agreed to hear him a second time. So Gerald returned to Wales to collect fresh evidence for his claim, only to discover that the Archbishop of Canterbury had already appointed the Abbot of St. Dogmaels to the See. This produced fresh difficulties, as the Abbot had been one of the original four nominees.

Gerald now became the butt of two contending factions. On the one hand, the Pope, anxious to have no break with the Archbishop of Canterbury, insisted that the Bishop-elect should have the unanimous support of the Chapter of St. David's. On the other, the Welsh canons were eager to remain on good terms with the king, and at that time John was very anxious not to anger the Pope. (He changed his mind later, but that was too late to help Gerald.) So the canons turned against their erstwhile champion, and, despite the support of Llywelyn Fawr, whom he had admired long ago as the boy who stood up to his uncles and obtained his rights, the election was quashed.

Gerald made a second journey to Rome in 1203, but, despite the fact that they exchanged entertaining anecdotes, Innocent refused to support his claim to the Bishopric. It was not in the interest of the Papacy, by that time engaged in a struggle with King John, to alienate the Archbishop of Canterbury. So Gerald returned to Wales, made peace with the Archbishop, and agreed to the election of the Prior of Llantony as Bishop in place of the Abbot of St. Dogmael's.

After this, Gerald retired from public life in Wales. He went to Lincoln, where he was able to pursue his academic work at his own pleasure. He published his books about Ireland and Wales, and followed them by a somewhat embittered history of the Angevin kings. He died in Lincoln in 1223, and was buried in his beloved St. David's.

Gerald's claim to fame does not lie in what he saw as his main objective, the independence of the Welsh Church, but in his delightful accounts of life in Wales during his own era. He wrote about himself and his country in a happy, unselfconscious way. He noted the kings and princes of his age, but was also an acute observer of ordinary things. His books give a complete picture of himself, contemporary events as he saw them, and life in Wales and abroad. But he also observed small, inconsequential things. For example, in his day beavers, although already becoming rare, could still be observed in some Welsh rivers. Gerald watched them in the Teivi River, and wrote:

> The Teivi has another singularity, being the only river in Wales or England which has beavers. . . . The beavers, in order to construct their castles in the middle of rivers, make use of animals of their own species instead of carts, who convey timber from the woods to the rivers. They entwine branches of willows with other wood, and elevate a kind of stage or scaffold, from which they may observe and watch the rising of the waters. . . . The animal can remain in or under the water at its pleasure, like the frog or the seal. They have short legs, broad bodies and stubbed tails. The beaver has but four teeth, two above and two below, broad and sharp like a carpenter's axe, and as such he uses them.

It is observations such as this which make Gerald of Wales a figure worth remembering. He would have preferred that his fight for the See of St. David's and the independence of the Welsh church should have gained him his place in the history of his country, but, from the point of view of the modern historian, his claim to fame lies in his description of contemporary life and his comments on the people he met, kings and Popes, Welsh princes and peasants. From his accounts it is possible to obtain an exact picture of everyday life in the early thirteenth century. Moreover, he had a tremendous sense of nationalism. The Welsh, he wrote, were often harassed and weakened by various attackers, not least the English. But, he declared, they would survive.

> Nor do I think that any other nation than that of Wales, nor any other language . . . shall, in the day of severe examination before the Supreme Judge, in any case answer for this corner of the earth.

Llywelyn The Great, 1173–1240

Llywelyn the Great

During the reigns of William of Normandy, his successors, and the first Plantaganets, Wales was—officially, at least—recognised as separate and independent from England. The Welsh language was used, Welsh laws, in particular the laws relating to inheritance, acknowledged, and the Welsh continued their tribal system of farming in family communities, ignoring the feudal system which now predominated in England. The dividing line between the two countries remained, roughly, the line of Offa's Dyke.

It was, however, impossible for the Welsh to maintain a purely separatist position, for various reasons. In the first place, the country had no supreme ruler. There were many local divisions, known as cantrefs and commotes, each the property of its own chieftain or 'prince'. Some of these princes also held land in England, for which they had to pay homage to the English king, and so in this respect they could be counted as his subjects. Moreover, on either side of Offa's Dyke lay a stretch of debatable ground, the Welsh March. This area was the scene of constant dispute; a string of Norman castles—Chester, Shrewsbury, Montgomery, Wigmore and Hay—had been built there by the Conqueror's Marcher Lords, whose function was to hold the Welsh back from attacking England. These Marcher Lords, on the other hand, were ambitious, and ready to take any opportunity which presented itself to seize Welsh land and add it to their feudal holdings. As a result, there existed a constant state of intermittent raids and inroads, with land constantly changing hands between the

Marcher Lords and the Welsh chieftains.

Of these latter, the most powerful were the Prince of Gwynedd, who held land in North Wales around the river Conway and the mountains of Snowdonia, the Prince of Powys, who ruled in Central Wales, and the Prince of Deheubarth, whose lands lay to the South. It was obviously to the advantage of the Marcher Lords and the English King to foster quarrels among these three chieftains and their followers, for, during a period of internal strife the Welsh would be in no position to make inroads across the border.

This was the situation in which Llywelyn ab Iorwerth rose to power in Wales. He was born at Nant Conway in 1173, and first became prominent in 1194, when he defeated his uncle, David, near Aberconwy. Under the Welsh law of inheritance, property was not inherited by the eldest son, but divided among the heirs of the previous holder, so Gwynedd had been shared between Iorwerth and David on the death of their father, Owain. Llywelyn realised that this system, carried to its logical conclusion, would eventually reduce the power of the ruling families of Wales to the point of impotence. Taking the English feudal law as his guide, he claimed his uncle's territory as the legal representative of the elder branch of the family, and before long made himself the supreme ruler of the whole of Gwynedd.

He soon came into conflict with the Lord of Powis, Gwenwynwyn, whose boundaries now touched his own. He also attracted the attention of the new king of England, John, who was anxious to prevent any of the Welsh princes from obtaining a paramount position. John knew the Welsh March, for as Earl of Gloucester he had had to deal with a border rebellion. Determined to check Llywelyn, he allied himself to Gwenwynwyn and promised him military aid. But he soon realised that Llywelyn would not be easy to dispose of: he was fighting on his own ground, and his Welsh followers were ready to make use of any opportunity to harass the hated Marcher Lords. Giraldus Cambrensis wrote of them: 'The defence of their native land and liberty is their only concern. They fight for their fatherland and they labour for liberty. They deem it . . . an honour to fall in the field of battle.'

In 1201, finding the support of Gwenwynwyn too costly, John concluded a treaty with Llywelyn. He promised not to oppose the prince in possession of his lands in Wales, and Llywelyn swore fealty to John in return. This seemed at first to be a reasonable arrangement, for John could not entirely trust his Marcher Lords to support him and in 1204 one of them, de Braose, fell into disgrace for plotting against the King. His estates were confiscated by the crown, and Gwenwynwyn, eager to revenge himself on John, proceeded to attack Builth and the surrounding area. Llywelyn, true to his oath, turned upon his rival and drove him out of the de Braose lands. He also pressed his advantage by seizing from the retreating Gwenwynwyn a considerable area of Powys. This John agreed that he should keep. As a further reward, he arranged a marriage between his youngest daughter, Joan, and Llywelyn, giving as her dowry the castle and manor of Ellesmere, in Shropshire.

Joan came to occupy a prominent place in the history of Wales. She was an illegitimate child, but seems to have been greatly loved by her father. Her husband, too, loved her dearly, and time and time again she appears as mediator between these two irascible personalities. Wise, tactful and serene, she was constantly in her husband's confidence. Only on one occasion did she fail him, and then, as subsequent events show, he forgave her, both because he loved her and because he was unable to rule his kingdom without relying on her counsel.

In 1209, Llywelyn accompanied John in

an expedition against the King of Scotland. In 1210, the King was at war in Ireland, and returned by way of South Wales, passing easily through Pembroke and Glamorgan, where the prince of Deheubarth offered no resistance. This was during the period when England lay under a Papal Interdict. John had quarrelled with Pope Innocent III, whose nominee, Stephen Langton, he refused to accept as Archbishop of Canterbury; Innocent retaliated by banning church services throughout the kingdom, excommunicating John, and, in 1211, releasing his lords from the obligations laid upon them by their oaths of fealty to him.

This put John in a very vulnerable position, for the oath of fealty was a serious matter and he was now left without any backing against a rebellious subject. He contemplated his son-in-law's territorial acquisitions from Powys and decided that he could not afford to let one man control so much of Wales; an alliance with any of the powerful Marcher Lords could possibly cost John his kingdom. So, in 1211 he assembled a strong army at Chester, determined to show Llywelyn that he was still a subject, in spite of his marriage to the king's daughter.

At first, John was surprised by the strength of the Welsh resistance. He had not anticipated the difficulties of fighting in mountainous terrain, where his heavily-armed knights fell an easy prey to Llywelyn's light-armed hill men. Before long, the king was forced to withdraw because he found it impossible to maintain his supply-lines.

Later in the year, however, he made a second attack, this time in conjunction with Gwenwynwyn. The armies met at Chester and made a joint advance along the river Conwy. Bangor was taken and burned to the ground and Llywelyn fled to his mountain fastness of Snowdonia. Realising that he could not defeat John, he arranged a meeting between princess Joan and her father, at

Snowdon from Lake Gwynant

which terms were made for what Llywelyn felt to be a shameful treaty. John took all of Llywelyn's land lying between Snowdonia and Chester, thus confining him to the estates which he had originally inherited from his father. Gwenwynwyn's lost territory was restored to him. John also imposed a heavy tribute and took thirty of Llywelyn's leading subjects as hostages. The fortunes of Gwynedd seemed to have touched their nadir, for Llywelyn had lost all he had fought for. And, as a crowning humiliation, John ordered the building of royal castles in Wales, at Aberystwyth and Caernarvon.

In the long run, these harsh terms did the king more harm than good. He should have known Llywelyn well enough to realise that he was not the man to submit tamely to such a situation for long. Moreover, the establishment of the royal castles inflamed the fierce national pride of the Welsh people who, even beyond his own lands, began to look to Llywelyn as their natural leader against this threat of English domination. Furthermore, John faced increasing difficulties in his own kingdom, of which Llywelyn was well aware. The prolongation of the Interdict had made the English restless; the barons chafed under his tyrannical rule, and the Pope backed them, urging the king of France to invade

England and depose John unless he agreed to accept Langton as Archbishop and accede to the barons' demands.

At this point, in 1212, Llywelyn took advantage of the situation. He persuaded all the Welsh princes, including his old rival Gwenwynwyn, to join him in a patriotic alliance with the avowed object of destroying the hated royal castles. A great Welsh army was massing on the western side of the March, while a French invasion and civil war threatened England. Faced with this situation, John submitted to the Pope. The Interdict was lifted, and with it the immediate threat of French invasion. In 1214 John made a truce with Wales, which gave Llywelyn all the land and power he wanted in his own country. Gwynedd became the supreme principality in Wales, and Llywelyn took the style and title of 'Prince of Aberffraw and Lord of Snowdon'.

John hoped for Llywelyn's help against his own barons but he did not get it. In 1215, the year of Magna Carta, Llywelyn backed them by taking the castle and town of Shrewsbury on their behalf. As a gesture of gratitude for his support, the barons agreed to acknowledge the supremacy of Welsh law throughout the Principality. Later, during the civil war in England, Llywelyn carried out his avowed intention of taking the royal castles, which quickly surrendered to his Welshmen, leaving the king without bases in Wales.

In 1216, John died. His heir, Henry III, was a minor, so the government was carried out by a council of state. An opportunity soon came for Llywelyn to demonstrate not only his ascendancy in Wales but also the independence of the principality. The prince of Deheubarth had died, leaving no direct issue; Llywelyn called a Welsh assembly to meet at Aberdovey to portion out South Wales amongst the various claimants. He presided over the assembly and guided their deliberations, but wisely refused to hold any territory in Deheubarth himself. This was government on the lines indicated in Magna Carta; the English, as he hoped, noticed his action and were impressed. Obviously, the Prince of Aberffraw was no wild guerilla chieftain but a civilised, well-informed ruler.

Llywelyn's relationship with his young brother-in-law began well. Not only was the prince confirmed in all his possessions, he was also granted formal custody of the royal castles of Cardigan and Carmarthen, to be maintained at his own expense until the king should be of age. His old enemy, Gwenwynwyn, was dead, and Llywelyn was made custodian of his lands, including Montgomery, until his several heirs became old enough to take charge of their property. At a solemn council held at Shrewsbury in 1221, David, his son by Joan, was recognised as his sole heir by the king, the justiciar (Hubert de Burgh) the Papal legate and the Archbishop of Canterbury. That same year, a marriage was arranged between his daughter, Helen, and the son of Earl Ranulf of Chester, one of the most powerful of the Marcher Lords; this alliance secured the north-eastern boundaries of Gwynedd.

Throughout the 1220s, there seems to have been a continued friendship between Henry III and Llywelyn, who met almost every year, usually when the king made a royal progress along the March and held court at Shrewsbury. In 1224 Llywelyn was given another English manor; he in his turn sent Henry a gift of hawks and falcons from Eryri. Two years later, princess Joan was declared legitimate by a Papal decree, and endowed by her half-brother with the manor of Condover, in Shropshire, to mark the occasion. At the end of the decade, Llywelyn attacked, in the name of the king, a rebellious Marcher Lord, William de Braose of Builth, and from this point the amicable family relationship began to deteriorate.

William de Braose was the son of the man who had quarrelled with John in 1204. The family appears to have produced Marcher Lords of a brigand type, ever ready to take advantage of local strife to increase their power. The outcome of Llywelyn's entanglement with this young man, however, was to be the great tragedy of his life, and it is interesting to speculate on the motives of the persons concerned.

Young William had rebelled against Henry, just when he was beginning—not very successfully—to take the government of England into his own hands. Llywelyn attacked him and took him prisoner, but his captivity does not appear to have been a very arduous one. He was allowed the freedom of the prince's manor—under escort, once he went outside the walls—and readily agreed to an arrangement whereby his daughter, Isabella, should marry Llywelyn's son, David. This marriage would be of advantage to both families, securing their boundaries in the same way as the alliance with the Earl of Chester had done. Llywelyn also demanded a high ransom, and this de Braose was prepared to pay. Then, the incredible happened. Joan, Llywelyn's honoured, beloved consort, was bewitched into a love affair with the prisoner, who was young enough to be her son. Llywelyn, returning unexpectedly from hunting, found them in bed together.

The infuriated husband, for the only time in his life, did not think or act like a statesman. He immediately hanged de Braose and imprisoned Joan. Public sympathy was with him; not one of his old enemies, the Marcher Lords, raised a finger to avenge de Braose. But Llywelyn, for the next eighteen months, seems to have acted without forethought, and this is a measure of the influence his wife had over him during all the years of their marriage. He insisted that the marriage contract between David and Isabella should stand, and left the de Braose estates severely

alone. But he made constant and unprovoked attacks on the March, burning towns, ravaging farms, and pressing over into England whenever he could. He gained nothing by this activity, and seemed likely to lose much that he already had. It seems a probability that at this juncture, having been betrayed by the person he loved most, he was indifferent to his future.

Henry, of course, sent troops to protect the English side of the March, and took the opportunity to subdue some of the Marcher Lords who resented his interference. His motives, too, are open to question. Had he, perhaps, resented Llywelyn through all the years of his minority, and was now only too pleased to meet him in open warfare? Was he sincerely attached to his half-sister and resentful of her punishment? It would be interesting to know more of these relationships, but contemporary records say very little of Joan's lapse. Llywelyn forgave her; he could not do without her, either as consort or as counsellor. In 1232 she was set free and restored to her former place of honour, and in 1234 a truce was made with King Henry.

This truce, known as the Pact of Middle because it was concluded at a point half-way between Shrewsbury and Ellesmere, put an end to warfare on the March for the rest of Llywelyn's lifetime. Its chief provisions stated that Llywelyn should keep all his conquests in Wales, and that neither he nor Henry should build new castles on either side of the March. He then returned in state to Wales, to spend the remaining years of his life in undisputed rule of the land that had become virtually his kingdom.

His reign was a period of enlightenment and marked a phase of artistic and scholarly achievement. He gathered about him a group of able men, among them his seneschal, Ednyfed Fychan, who was a direct ancestor of the Tudor kings. He encouraged the Celtic tradition in building and in literature;

churches and monasteries were erected, and he welcomed many new religious orders, giving equal freedom to the Franciscans, the Cistercians and the Canons of Ynys Lannog, who were anchorites of the very early Christian type, belonging to no recognised religious group but living as solitary hermits in caves or huts on the mountainside. He granted charters to the Cistercians at Cymer and Aberconwy, permitting the order to build new abbeys.

Snowdonia, Llywelyn's mountain fastness

When Joan died at Aber in 1237, he caused a new burial place to be enclosed on the island of Anglesey, where a house of Franciscan Friars was established to pray for the repose of her soul. Probably he intended this to become a royal burial place for the house of Gwynedd, and some of his descendants were interred there, although he himself was not.

The use of Welsh law was enforced throughout Llywelyn's territory despite the fact that he himself had conveniently ignored its ruling on inheritance. Traditionally, the laws of Wales had been promulgated by one Hywel Dda, but in the course of time variations had grown up in different districts. Early in the thirteenth century the first written version of Hywel Dda's laws was made, and this version, known as the Venedotian Code, was the one accepted by Llywelyn as the official law of Gwynedd.

Welsh literature flourished during Llywelyn's reign, and his court became a centre for bards, all of whom praised him. One, Einion ap Gwgon, sang of him:

He to me as the crystal mind,
I to him as the hand and eye.

Another, Prydydd y Moch, praises the wealth and generosity of his prince:

Well known is it that thy long hand never falters
As it bestows the red and yellow gold.
God made thee braver than any man that breathes,
Most liberal, too, as far as the sun's course extends.

The earliest written version of the Four Branches of the Mabinogion, a collection of the traditional legends and folk-lore of Wales, was made during Llywelyn's reign.

Llywelyn died in 1240, in his 67th year— a good age for a fighting-man of the early mediaeval period. When he knew that death was approaching, he was taken to the abbey at Aberconwy, where he died and, according to tradition, was buried wearing the habit of a lay-brother. Although he himself never used the title, he could well be called the first Prince of Wales, for he was the first man to unite the entire principality as one kingdom, and for this reason is aptly known to history as Llywelyn the Great, or, in his native language, Llywelyn Fawr.

Owain Glyndwr, *c.* 1359–1417

Owain Glyndwr

In 1283 David, the last native-born Prince of Wales, was captured in battle and executed at Shrewsbury. As a result, the Welsh lost the last vestige of their legal independence from England. Before the Norman Conquest, they had acknowledged their own princes, each ruling a small 'kingdom', their own language, laws and churches. After the Conquest, the powerful Lords of the March, planted by the Norman Kings to keep order on the debatable frontier ground between England and Wales began to thrust westwards, establishing castles and territorial holdings at such centres as Cardiff, Brecon, Abergavenny and Neath. They introduced the Norman system of manorial farming, but their Welsh tenants clung obstinately to their traditional manner of living and farming in family groups.

They hated the imposition of foreign rule, and in certain areas—Deheubarth in the south, Powys in the centre and Gwynedd in the north-west of the country—there were frequent rebellions. The princes of Gwynedd, in particular, constantly harried the Anglo-Norman rulers, and David of Wales was the last of the princes of Gwynedd. After his death, Edward I took possession of his lands and reinforced the great castles at Caernarvon, Conway and Harlech to hold the Welsh in check, so that for a century Welshmen were obliged to accept English rule.

Edward did not, however, attempt to abolish the use of Welsh language and literature, and many Welshmen served willingly in his wars against Scotland and France. But the majority loathed their status as a subject nation, and the Welsh bards sang frequently of one of the prophecies of Merlin, that a great leader would arise, who would not only restore independence to the Welsh but give them power over the whole of England, which they had lost at the time of the Saxon invasions. In 1378 a descendant of the Princes of Gwynedd, Owen of the Red Hand, declared himself to be the true Prince of Wales. He was murdered before he could give the English much trouble, but some poets, among them the great Iolo Goch, began to speak of another Owen who would complete his work. By 1400, when Owain Glyndwr first set himself up as a leader of the Welsh, the people were ready to follow him against the English King.

Owain Glyndwr (his name means 'Owen of the Valley of the Waters') was a descendant of the princes of Powys. His father held land in Glyndyfrdwy and Cynllaith. Here, not far from the Shropshire border, stood the chief house of the family, Sycharth, where Owain was born, probably in 1359—the exact date is not known.

His father, Griffith, was a land-owner of considerable wealth. When Owain was a youth, he was sent to be 'an apprentice of the law at Westminster', where he is likely to have spent seven years. In this way, he gained a thorough knowledge of English law and government which, combined with his inherent grounding in Welsh customs, was to prove of great value to him later.

Having completed his legal training, Owain became a squire, learning the rules of chivalry and courtly behaviour. He was eventually knighted, for a poet speaks of him as overthrowing a hundred knights in a tournament, 'resplendent in gold and scarlet trappings'. Strangely enough, the lord under whom he served was Henry of Lancaster, the eldest son of John of Gaunt. In later years, as Henry IV, Lancaster was destined to become Owain's mortal enemy. The two men gained their military experience in the same wars,

fighting for Edward III and Richard II in Scotland and in France. Welsh poets give a vivid description of Owain during the Scottish campaign of 1385. One says that he wore 'a scarlet feather in his shining helmet'; another tells of him driving the Scots before him while 'they howled with fear'. Iolo Goch, his personal bard, already had a vision of him as a born leader, destined to awaken the sleeping soul of Wales.

The great seal of Owain Glyndwr

Owain married Margaret Hanmer, the daughter of one of Edward III's judges. Though of English descent, her father, Sir David Hanmer, held land in North Wales and had a great admiration for Welsh culture. Owain inherited Sycharth on his father's death, and here he and his wife brought up six sons and four daughters. They were wealthy, and lived in considerable splendour, entertaining men of culture, both Welsh and English. Iolo Goch describes Sycharth as 'a fair wooden house, standing upon four wondrous pillars on the crest of a green hill'. It had a great chimney, many rooms, a courtyard, and was surrounded by meadows, cornfields, orchards and good hunting country.

At this period, Owain appeared to be a settled country landowner, more concerned with the management of his estate than with national affairs. But Iolo Goch and other bards constantly sang of the great leader who was destined to throw off the English yoke. Despite his English education Owain was a nationalist at heart, and gradually he began to feel that he was the man to succeed where the Princes of Gwynedd had failed a hundred years earlier.

In 1399, Richard II was deposed by Henry of Lancaster, who became King Henry IV. Richard had been popular in Wales, despite the fact that the Welsh had been heavily taxed in order to finance his foreign wars. Henry IV levied even heavier taxes, and this caused great resentment, especially as his claim to the throne was of a dubious nature. There were rumours of rebellions in parts of North Wales and attempts to plot with Scotland, the traditional enemy of the English Crown. In 1400, Lord Grey of Ruthin sought from the King permission to take drastic action against leaders of riots and their relatives, for as a Marcher Lord he understood very well the tribal loyalties of the Welsh.

At this time, Lord Grey became involved in a legal battle with Owain Glyndwr. Grey had taken possession of a piece of land belonging to Owain. Owain, trained in English law, brought a suit against him and finally asked the Parliament which met early in 1400 to arbitrate in the matter. The Commons refused to hear him, so he went to the King. But Henry could not afford to quarrel with Lord Grey, whose claim he upheld. Owain returned to Wales with a deep sense of injustice, and he was not the only Welshman with a grudge of this nature; there was a feeling that the scales of justice were invariably weighted in favour of the English.

In September 1400 Owain, his brother and his eldest son met a number of leading Welshmen at Glyndyfrdwy. They proclaimed Owain Prince of Wales and urged him to lead them against Lord Grey. In a series of rapid attacks Ruthin, Denbigh, Rhuddlan, Flint and Oswestry were plundered before the rebels were scattered by an English force.

Henry IV learned of this revolt when returning from an attack upon Scotland.

Seriously alarmed, he made a detour, leading the royal army through North Wales. He confiscated the estates of the ringleaders, Owain's among them, with the result that these men spent the ensuing winter as fugitives.

Had he paused to enquire in detail into the problems of the Welsh, Henry might at this point have won them over, but he did not. On the advice of Lord Grey and other Marcher Lords, the Parliament of 1401 passed laws forbidding Welshmen to trade or to hold property in any English township, especially those on the March; Welshmen were to be tried by English law, in English courts; the bards were declared 'vagabonds'. As a result, in 1401 the rebellion broke out afresh.

Owain, now acclaimed as the national leader by common consent, attacked in South Wales, and was so successful that he was expected to press on into England. Instead, he turned north and besieged Caernarvon Castle, but was unable to take the fortress. He sought help from the King of Scotland, but, getting no response, pressed on alone, in 1402 taking captive Lord Grey himself.

By this time, Henry IV realised that an experienced campaigner was needed to deal with the Welsh revolt. He appointed the son of the Earl of Northumberland, Lord Henry Percy—Shakespeare's Hotspur—to subdue Glyndwr. But before he could act, Owain attacked in Radnorshire, defeated an English army at Bryn Glas, and took another important prisoner, Edmund Mortimer, Earl of March. He now had in his hands two men of immense political significance—Lord Grey, the King's friend, and Edmund Mortimer, whose claim to the throne was by many people considered to be more valid than that of Henry himself.

In the autumn, Henry personally led an army into Wales to capture Owain. But the weather fought against him. Day after day it rained; the Severn flooded and a low mist perpetually shrouded the hills. The royal army, lost in the wild country, frequently stumbled into the floods where men and horses were drowned, while light-armed Welsh guerillas emerged suddenly from the mist to attack stragglers. The English were terrified of Owain, whom they were convinced was a wizard in league with the devil to conjure up these terrible conditions; Henry was forced to withdraw.

He was, however, prepared to negotiate for Grey's release, and Parliament agreed to pay a large proportion of the ransom. At the same time, a number of stringent anti-Welsh laws were passed, forbidding Welshmen to bear arms unless in the King's service, prohibiting the tenure of offices under the crown by Welshmen, and virtually outlawing any Englishman who married any female kin of Owain Glyndwr.

Mortimer was not ransomed; it was obviously to Henry's advantage for him to be kept out of England, so that he was in no position to challenge the King. Realising this, the Earl made an alliance with Owain and married one of his daughters. He also opened negotiations on Owain's behalf with Hotspur, who was his sister's husband, with the result that the latter changed his allegiance and joined Owain and Mortimer in open revolt against Henry. Hotspur won a promise of aid from his father, the powerful Earl of Northumberland.

Immediately, Henry took action to prevent a joint attack by these dangerous allies. In 1403 he caught up with Hotspur's army at Shrewsbury, where Hotspur was defeated and killed. But though this victory was a great gain to Henry, it made little difference to Glyndwr's strength in Wales. Later in the year, he took four of Henry's castles— Llanstephan, Newcastle Emlyn, Dryslwyn and Carreg Cennen—and encouraged Breton pirates to attack English supply ships, so that the garrisons of Harlech and Caernarvon became short of food. Before the end of 1403 he had captured Cardiff Castle, and was able to spend the rest of the winter in preparation for a major onslaught in the following spring.

Early in 1404, Owain took both Harlech and Aberystwyth castles. He thus became sufficiently powerful to establish himself as ruler of the whole of central Wales, from the coast of Cardigan Bay as far eastward as the territories of the most powerful of the Marcher lords. He summoned a Parliament of Wales to meet at Machynlleth, where plans were formulated for the government of the Principality as an independent state.

Assuming the title 'Prince of Wales', Owain adopted the old royal arms of the Princes of Gwynedd. Through his brother-in-law, John Hanmer, and his chancellor, Griffith Young, he negotiated a treaty with the King of France, uniting both 'against Henry of Lancaster, adversary and enemy of both parties'. The French were already allies of the Scots; if an attack came from across the Channel the English would be forced to fight on three fronts, and in the prospect of this division lay Owain's hope of winning the whole of Wales. But his grand design was doomed to failure. Although a force of ships set sail for England, the French wasted a considerable amount of time and energy in minor skirmishes with the English up and down the Channel. Three landings were made on the south coast, but came to nothing. The Bretons, Scots and Welsh seemed incapable of a combined effort, and it was obvious that Owain must continue to act alone, aiming always for the establishment of an independent Principality of Wales.

Owain was reluctant, however, to abandon his plan to remove Henry IV from the English throne, and early in 1405 he embarked upon a scheme in favour of the Mortimer heir. This alliance, known as the Tri-partite Indenture, proposed a division of

Glyndwr's Parliament House, Machynlleth

the countries amongst the parties, Owain, Edmund Mortimer and the Earl of Northumberland, father of Hotspur. This arrangement is discussed, somewhat inaccurately, in Shakespeare's *Henry IV, Part I*. The Mortimers were to receive Southern England and the crown, Northumberland the North and the Midlands, while Owain was to have Wales and a large part of England,

> 'from the Severn Sea . . . to the north gate of the city of Worcester, and from that gate to the Ash Tree . . . on the highway leading from Bridgnorth to Kynvar; thence by the highway . . . to the head or source of the Trent; thence to the head or source of the river commonly called the Mersey, thence as that river leads to the sea.'

Geographically, this seems a strange area to be ruled by Wales, but Owain had several good reasons for his demands. The territory included Worcester, Hereford and Shrewsbury, the principal launching-grounds for attacks against Wales; it would enable him to protect Welsh settlers in the various border towns, and it would ensure him bases in England from which he could, should the need arise, prepare an armed force to meet the unreliable Earl of Northumberland on reasonably equal terms.

The alliance with France was also renewed, and at the beginning of August 1405, Owain summoned a Welsh Parliament to Harlech castle. They voted to provide him with men and money, and he set out at the head of an army ten thousand strong, to unite with a French force which landed at Milford Haven. They easily captured Haverfordwest and Carmarthen, then pushed into English territory until they were within eight miles of Worcester—the largest army since the Norman Conquest to penetrate so great a distance into the kingdom.

It seemed as if Owain's dream was at last to be realised, but the great adventure came to nothing. There was no battle, nor did Henry sue for peace; indeed, he virtually ignored the invasion, and at the beginning of winter most of the French force returned home, while Owain retired to Wales. It seems strange that Henry IV took no action; perhaps he made use of his knowledge of Owain's temperament. The two men had known one another well in their young days, and had been on several campaigns together. It is possible that Henry realised that nothing would be more unbearable to Owain than such an anti-climax to the massive preparations for what he must have expected to result in the culmination of his hopes. Henry, on the other hand, was of a more phlegmatic temperament and it suited him well to bide his time.

He did, however, follow Owain into Wales during the wet spring of 1406. Again, the weather was on the side of the Welsh and floods, gales and mountain mists forced Henry to withdraw, leaving in Owain's hands his entire baggage train, consisting of weapons, valuables and food. A temporary truce was arranged, both sides hoping to gain time to prepare for a summer campaign. But for Owain, the period of his greatest success was over.

Although there was no open break with the French, it was obvious that he could not count on their further support. He did, however, enter into negotiations with the Pope at Avignon, Benedict XIII. This was the period of the dual papacy, and an agreement would have had the effect of making St. David's a metropolitan church, its bishop to rank equally with the Archbishop of Canterbury. Owain also planned to establish two universities, one in North Wales, the other in the South. He was in many ways a man in advance of his time. Had he been in a position to augment this policy, Wales would have become a centre of learning equal in importance to Oxford or Paris. But, like the great invasion of England in the previous year, his design came to nothing.

Circumstances were against Owain after 1406. His French allies left him, and Henry IV defeated not only the Earl of Northumberland but also the Scots, whose child-king became his prisoner and remained in England for the next eighteen years. For the first time since Richard II's death, Lancaster was firmly entrenched as King of England, only the Welsh remaining obdurate. And some of them were beginning to lose enthusiasm for the struggle; Gower in the south and Anglesey in the north submitted to the English, and the young Prince of Wales, later to become the warrior-king Henry V, demanded from Parliament authority to crush the rebellion.

By 1407 the tide was turning. Henry, now his position was secure, was able to give his full attention to the disaffection in Wales. And young Prince Henry, a born general, made full use of the weakness of his enemy. Supplied by sea, the strongest English castles in Wales withstood Welsh siege. Prince Henry, moreover, was well equipped with superior weapons. He used cannon against Owain's strongholds. These unexpected weapons were brought overland from Yorkshire to Bristol, and then ferried by sea to the Cardigan coast. Owain was not beaten yet, but the end of the struggle was in sight.

From 1407 to 1408, Aberystwyth castle held out against Prince Henry, but in the summer the garrison surrendered. That same year, Harlech was taken, and Owain's wife, two of his daughters and some of his many grandchildren became captives and were imprisoned in London, though Owain, his son Meredith and several other Welsh leaders managed to escape. But he was no longer a ruling prince: the heart had gone out of the majority of his subjects and he was now nothing more than a rebellious fugitive.

Even so, he would not give up. Two more attacks were made on the Shropshire border, one in 1410 and another in 1412. The English were so uncertain as to the real degree of power that remained to him that the whole of the March had to be kept in a state of readiness. In 1411 alone, the pay for the soldiers defending the border was one of the main items of expenditure listed by the royal exchequer. But Owain was ageing, and he had to deal with a foe younger than his own sons, already a warrior of considerable repute. In 1413, Henry IV died, and in 1415 Henry V offered a free pardon to all Welsh rebels who would yield to him. Owain, who was mentioned in the decree by name, refused, preferring to go into hiding.

What was his final end, no-one knows. He simply disappeared, and by 1417 was probably dead. It is most likely that he went to his daughter, Alice, and her husband, John Scudamore, who had a manor at Monnington Straddel in the Golden Valley. There is a strong tradition that he spent his old age with them, but nothing is recorded of his death or place of burial.

Owain's protracted rebellion was the last great attempt by the Welsh to separate themselves from English rule. For Wales, it was an economic disaster, for it took another generation before trade and rebuilding could become effective, while harsh laws were passed to ensure the subjection of the Principality. Enmity continued between Welsh and English, and in many cases between Welshman and Welshman, for those who had fought with Owain felt bitter contempt for those who had not. Owain himself, however, was remembered as an inspiring leader, a nationalist who had done for his fellow-countrymen what William Wallace had done for Scotland and Joan of Arc for France. He provided a source of inspiration for

Henry IV—an effigy in Canterbury Cathedral

Welshmen which is remembered even to-day, although so little is known of him as a person.

Obviously, he must have possessed a great power of leadership and the ability to arouse the loyalty of men. Even when his fortunes reached their lowest ebb, and he was in hiding with a price on his head, no-one ever betrayed him to his enemies. Yet there exists no authentic portrait of him, and records of his actual words are few. Legends quickly gathered about his name; the English firmly believed him to be a wizard, in league with the Devil. (They said the same of Joan of Arc!) But his mystique persisted, so that to this day he is recognised as one of those who gave Wales its separate entity. Almost a century after his death, when Henry Tudor, another Welshman, became king of England, many of his countrymen felt his accession to be the culmination of Owain's work for Wales. A legend, told by Ellis Griffith, a Tudor chronicler, points to this as a contemporary opinion. Griffith relates a story that Owain, out walking early one morning, met the Abbot of Valle Crucis, in the foothills of the Berwyns.

'You are up betimes, Master Abbot,' was Owain's greeting. 'Nay sire, it is you who have risen too soon,' replied the Abbot, 'and by a century.'

So a Welshman of Tudor days referred to the heritage bequeathed by an earlier leader.

Henry Tudor, 1457–1509

Henry Tudor, a portrait bust by Torrigiano

Ever since the Norman Conquest, with its subsequent inroads upon Welsh territory, the bards of Wales had sung of a prince who would fulfil the ancient prophecies attributed to Merlin, restoring all Britain to the rule of a Celt.

Bards had always held an important place in the history of Wales. More than musicians, less than priests, theirs were the mystic voices which kept Celtic culture, Celtic traditions and Celtic laws alive at a time when the English Marcher Lords were encroaching into the Principality and making every effort to stamp out nationalism. The bards were revered by the people and honoured by the princes. Llywelyn Fawr, Llywelyn the Last and Owain Glyndwr maintained their own personal bards in their maenols as respected counsellors. And in Henry Tudor, the Welshman who became England's last mediaeval monarch, the words of Merlin seemed finally to be justified.

Henry was the heir of that era of civil strife known to history as the Wars of the Roses. His immediate ancestry linked him to the royal house of Plantaganet, although he had no direct claim to the throne. Margaret Beaufort, his mother, was the great-granddaughter of Edward III's son, John of Gaunt, by his marriage to Catherine Swynford. Catherine, whose sister, Phillipa, was the wife of the poet Chaucer, was a woman of great beauty who had been for many years Gaunt's mistress. After the death of his second wife, Constanza, Queen of Castile, he married her, and by a special decree enacted during Richard II's reign all their children were

Lady Margaret Beaufort, mother of Henry Tudor

Tudor by name, became one of the King's pages and, because of his gallantry on the field of Agincourt, was promoted to the rank of Squire of the Body to the King. Doubtless he would have been knighted had Henry lived, but when the young king died Owen was little known outside the royal household, where he remained as Clerk of the Wardrobe to the Queen-Dowager, Katherine de Valois. Katherine was young and lonely, forced by circumstances to remain in England although her child, the baby Henry VI, was cared for by a succession of governesses and tutors appointed by the Regent, so that his mother seldom saw him. She was attracted by her Welsh servant, and tradition has it that Owen Tudor was a man of unusual charm. In 1425 they were married, though the wedding was of necessity a secret one, since dire penalties threatened any man who married the Queen without the consent of the Council of Regency.

For eleven years they lived together, apparently in great happiness, and Katherine gave birth to five Tudor children, of whom two, Jasper and Edmund, were of paramount importance to the future king. But in 1436 the storm broke. The marriage was discovered, the couple forcibly separated. Queen Katherine was sent to Bermondsey Abbey, where she died within a year; her children were cared for by the nuns of Barking. Owen, terrified by the consequences of his action, sought sanctuary in Westminster Abbey. He was promised a safe-conduct to Wales and surrendered, only to find himself placed under arrest in Newgate prison. However, he managed to escape and returned to Anglesey, where he remained unmolested until Henry VI came of age.

The King respected his mother's memory and showed great kindness to his stepfather and half-brothers, who in their turn were unswervingly loyal to the Lancastrian cause. Owen and his second son, Jasper, fought for

declared legitimate, although with the proviso that none should ever succeed to the English crown. Nevertheless the blood of the Plantaganets flowed in the veins of Margaret Beaufort and, as her long, narrow features and delicate hands show, she resembled them, and passed on this resemblance to her own great-granddaughter, Elizabeth I.

When Henry Tudor became Henry VII of England, he boasted of his Welsh ancestry and had the heralds prepare for him a very elaborate pedigree in which he traced his line back to such mythical personalities as King Arthur and Cadwallader the Great. He was certainly descended, through his father, from Ednyfed Vaughan, Llywelyn Fawr's seneschal, but the story of his grandfather is of more interest than that of any of his more remote forebears.

During the brief reign of Henry V, a Welsh gentleman from Anglesey, Owen

Henry at the battle of Mortimer's Cross, where the Lancastrians were defeated. Jasper escaped, but his father was beheaded at Hereford. His last words were: 'That head shall lie on the block that was wont to lie on Queen Katherine's lap.' Jasper and his brother Edmund were determined to avenge their father's death.

They had been declared legitimate by Act of Parliament and the elder, Edmund, was created Earl of Richmond, while Jasper became Earl of Pembroke. At the especial wish of Henry VI, who was a kindly man of strong family feeling, Edmund Tudor married the orphaned Lady Margaret Beaufort, a girl of thirteen, scholarly and possessed of unusual intelligence and personality. But the misfortunes of the civil war brought the marriage to an abrupt end, for Edmund was captured by the Yorkists in South Wales and imprisoned in Carmarthen Castle, where he died. This was in 1456, and his young wife was already expecting her first child.

Jasper took the girl—she had not yet had her fourteenth birthday—to the safety of Pembroke Castle, where on 28 January 1457, her son was born. He was given the name of Henry, after his uncle the King, and later succeeded to his father's title as Earl of Richmond. Although his mother twice re-married he remained her only child, and she and his uncle, Jasper of Pembroke, were the main influences of his formative years. It was on her descent from the House of Lancaster that he was later to base his claim to the throne.

When Henry was four years old, Pembroke Castle was seized by the Yorkists. The child was separated from his mother—who had by now remarried—and from his uncle, and placed under the guardianship of the new owner of the castle, William Herbert. Herbert showed him great kindness and supervised his education; it must have been a shock to the child when, in 1469, his guardian was executed on the orders of the Earl of Warwick. But the following year, with the restoration of Henry VI, Jasper Tudor was able to take his twelve-year-old nephew to court. It was Henry's first visit to England. He was presented to the King, who was so impressed by the boy's impeccable demeanour that he observed: 'This, truly, is he unto whom both we and our adversaries must yield and give over the dominion.' Future events proved his strange words to be true.

The year 1471 saw the Yorkists once again in power, and Jasper Tudor fled with his nephew to the safety of Brittany, helped by some citizens of Pembroke to take ship at Tenby. They remained in Brittany for several years, for after the deaths of Henry VI and his son, Henry Tudor became the only Lancastrian heir, and a source of potential danger to both Edward IV and his brother, Richard III. Henry's mother, who had by now married her third husband, Lord Stanley, remained in England. She wrote frequently to her son, however, and was already anxious to bring about his marriage to Edward IV's eldest daughter, Elizabeth of York.

In 1483 a rebellion broke out against Richard III, led by the Duke of Buckingham, who invited Henry Tudor to come to England and deliver the kingdom from tyranny. Henry came, but storms delayed his arrival, and it was soon obvious that, except in Wales, he would have little support. Welshmen identified his cause with the cause of Wales, and the most popular of the bards, David Llwyd ap Llywelyn of Machynlleth, hailed him as the man who would rescue the Welsh from Saxon domination. But Henry prudently withdrew in the face of Richard's superior power, though his solemn oath to marry Princess Elizabeth of York when he became King of England pleased the Welsh, for she was descended from Llywelyn Fawr through the Mortimer line.

Two years later, however, Henry Tudor attacked Richard again, and this time he was successful. Landing at Milford Haven with an army of Lancastrians reinforced by French mercenaries, he marched through the Prescelly Mountains eastward to Machynlleth, where he was joined by an army of Welshmen under Rhys ap Thomas. On they went, through the Midlands until they met Richard's army at Bosworth. There the Lancastrians were victorious, Richard was killed, and the protracted strife known as the Wars of the Roses ended when the new King, Henry VII, was acclaimed. He was the first ruler of the Tudor dynasty.

Of course, his accession did not go unchallenged. The claim of the young Earl of Warwick, Edward IV's nephew, who was a descendant of both the Mortimer line and of Edward III's second son, Lionel, was a stronger one. And no one knew for certain that Edward's two sons had died in the Tower. But Henry Tudor was undoubtedly a Plantaganet. More important, he was a strong man who offered the kingdom peace after the prolonged civil war. The majority of his subjects accepted him with gratitude.

After his coronation, he fulfilled his promise to marry Edward's daughter, Elizabeth of York, and the wedding took place at Westminster in January 1486. The princess, twenty years old, was eight years younger than her husband, and had inherited the good looks of both her parents, being tall, with wide-set hazel eyes, golden hair and a fair skin. The marriage, though essentially one of diplomacy, arranged to unite the houses of York and Lancaster, developed into a very happy one. Elizabeth bore seven children, only three of whom were destined to outlive her. She died at thirty-eight, after giving birth to her last child, a girl who survived her by only two days. Henry, who had loved her devotedly

for seventeen years, was inconsolable. The gaiety which had marked the court during her lifetime vanished, and, although he considered making another marriage for reasons of policy, he never did so.

Elizabeth of York, daughter of Edward IV and wife of Henry Tudor. Their marriage united the houses of York and Lancaster

Henry VII's reign began auspiciously, although his first years as king were troubled by threats from pretenders whose claims were even weaker than his own. His people longed for peace, and his first Parliament passed an Act declaring that the inheritance of the crown belonged by right to him and to his heirs but this did not prevent opposition. The stories of Lambert Simnel and of Perkin Warbeck are well known; both were pawns used by Henry's enemies. Simnel impersonated the feeble-minded Earl of Warwick, who was imprisoned in the Tower, and some Yorkist supporters were ready enough to hail him as 'Edward VI'. Supported by Richard III's friend, Lord Lovell, he came over from Ireland with an army of mercenaries financed by Margaret of Burgundy, the sister of Richard III and Edward IV. Henry defeated them at Stoke, where most of the surviving Yorkist leaders were killed. Simnel was treated with lenience; he was sent to work in the king's kitchen, and lived to become the Royal Falconer and a loyal servant of the Tudors. Henry was never given to unnecessary bloodshed.

The Battle of Stoke was of greater importance than the Battle of Bosworth in establishing the Tudor dynasty. Perkin Warbeck's attempt to pass himself off as the younger son of Edward IV gained very little support in England, although he was a source of trouble to Henry for six years, working from abroad. Once again, Margaret of Burgundy backed the false claimant, as did the King of Scotland, but neither really believed him to be the Prince. When captured, he was imprisoned in the Tower and had every chance of being treated as well as Lambert Simnel. However, he continued to plot against the Crown and was executed.

Henry Tudor did not forget his Welsh ancestry and honoured his Welsh kinsfolk. His uncle, Jasper Tudor, who had sheltered him during his childhood, was created Earl of Bedford. Jasper had recently married the widow of the Duke of Buckingham, who had by her first marriage a young son, born at Brecon Castle during the civil war. Henry restored the Dukedom to the boy, Edward Stafford, and appointed Jasper his guardian. The child was often at court, where Henry treated him as a son.

Henry's stepfather, Lord Stanley, third husband of Lady Margaret Beaufort, was also rewarded for his part in helping Henry to become king. He was made Earl of Derby and at Henry's coronation he acted as Lord High Steward. Later, he stood godfather to Henry's eldest son. Lady Margaret herself sought no honours; it was sufficient that her only son was now King of England. In his turn, he never ceased to confide in her, and it was due to her love of learning and the arts that the English court welcomed so many scholars and humanists.

Henry VII was the first English monarch to bring about a genuine union of England and Wales. Jasper Tudor governed South Wales until his death, when Rhys ap Thomas of Dynevor was appointed Justice and Chamberlain in his place. Welshmen were given government posts in the Principality, others were encouraged to come to court. One became a captain of the Yeomen of the Guard; his grandson became Lord Burghley when Elizabeth I was queen. Some came from Wales to trade; Edward ap Rhys opened a brewery, known as 'The Welshman', in Fleet Street. The powers of the Marcher Lords gradually disappeared, for laws were passed forbidding barons to maintain large private armies. There was to be no repetition of the Wars of the Roses.

Always mindful of the support the Welsh had given him on the way to Bosworth, Henry encouraged Welsh national pride and always emphasised his own Welsh blood. He frequently used the Red Dragon of Wales as a supporter to his own personal coat of arms. When his eldest son was born, he was christened Arthur, a name evocative of all the heroism of Welsh folklore, for had not the legendary Arthur been 'King of all Britain'?

Young Arthur was known as 'the hope of Britain', and certainly all Henry's hopes for the future of the Tudor dynasty were centred on this, his eldest child. At the age of three the boy was created Prince of Wales, and in that same year, 1489, it was arranged by the Treaty of Medina del Campo that he should eventually marry Catherine, the youngest daughter of Ferdinand and Isabella of Spain. The betrothal of these children, which was followed by a proxy marriage, was a great coup for Henry. Spain was the most powerful kingdom in Europe; the prospect of marriage to a Spanish princess demonstrated that the Tudors were not considered to be upstarts, but accepted as the English royal house. The fact that Ferdinand and Isabella recognised this was largely due to the Spanish ambassador, de Peubla, who emphasised the advantages of the alliance, pointing to the fact that, under Henry, the kingdom had rapidly recovered from the economic disasters of civil war and was becoming one of the wealthiest trading nations in the world. However, it was not until twelve years later that Catherine came to England.

Meanwhile, Prince Arthur had to learn statecraft, and Henry arranged that he should do so in his own Principality. The Council of the Welsh Marches, appointed by Edward IV though in abeyance during the Wars of the Roses, was revived. This Council, which consisted of both Welsh and English landowners, administered the affairs, of Wales. It met at Ludlow Castle, and young Arthur, from the age of six, had to attend lengthy meetings over which he was, of course, too young to preside. Ludlow was a convenient centre for both Welsh and English, and it was to Ludlow Castle that Arthur and Catherine were sent after their marriage, in 1501. He was fifteen, she a year or two older. They were hailed as Prince and Princess of Wales, and all the local gentry came to the castle to greet them. Feasting and tournaments continued for a month; the people of Wales were very conscious of the fact that to them had been sent the future King and Queen of the land.

But in March 1502 there was an influenza epidemic in Ludlow, and Prince Arthur caught the infection and died. Catherine was a widow, Henry and Elizabeth heartbroken, and all the people mourned. Arthur was buried in a magnificent tomb in Worcester Cathedral, and Rhys Nanmor, most prominent of bards, wrote a lament for him. True, Henry had another son, named after himself; it is odd that he never showed so much interest and pride in the future Henry VIII as he had in the delicate Arthur.

The following year, Henry lost his wife, and from then his way of life changed. During her lifetime, the English court had been one of the most magnificent in Europe. Although he later gained the reputation of being a miser, Henry delighted in rich clothes for himself and his suite. His personal bodyguard wore tunics of scarlet velvet and flat black caps; the other household servants were dressed in white and green. He had a true Welshman's love of music, having at his court a body of musicians as well as a chapel choir, while his household accounts mention payments to 'makers of organs and clavichords'. One day, riding through Canterbury, he heard a group of children singing near a meadow. Their songs gave him so much pleasure that he rewarded them with a gift of forty pence—as much as a journeyman would earn in a week. The courtiers often took part in masques and pageants.

But the court became more sombre after the death of the Queen. For a time, Henry took refuge in solitude and 'would that no man should resort unto him'. Later, he returned to the business of the kingdom— he even at one time contemplated a second marriage—but the light-heartedness was gone. Instead of musicians, scholars were welcomed to his court. His mother's love of learning probably had some influence here. Erasmus frequently visited England, where he met such friends as Colet, Dean of St. Pauls, and Thomas More. An Italian scholar, Polydore Vergil, made his home in England and was asked by Henry to compile a history of the country. He discarded myths about Arthur and King Lud, and worked from facts as he knew them. His narrative of Henry's own early years and the events of the Wars of the Roses came from contemporary sources, and in relating earlier events he frequently discarded the sometimes biased accounts of the monastic chronicles.

During an era of great discoveries, England lagged behind. Merchants were more concerned with trade than with the New World, but in 1498 John Cabot, with a crew of men from Bristol, sailed west and discovered 'The New Found Land'. It is interesting to note that the Bristol men on their return announced jubilantly that they could 'bring thence so many fish that they would have no further need of Iceland'. Even in those days, the presence of a British fishing fleet in Icelandic waters caused resentment.

If he were remembered for nothing else, Henry would have a lasting monument in the beautiful Gothic chapel which he caused to be erected in Westminster Abbey. It was originally intended as a shrine for the bones of Henry VI, who had always shown kindness to the Tudors. Henry hoped to persuade the Pope to canonise Henry VI, but this did not come to pass. So the chapel was completed as a resting-place for the founders of the Tudor dynasty. Here may be seen the effigies of Henry VII and his queen, decorated with embossed Tudor roses. Here, too, lies Margaret Beaufort, who outlived her son by a year. The tombs, sculptured by the Italian, Pietro Torrigiano, are guarded by cherubs and watched by a stone dragon of Wales. Even in death, Henry Tudor was mindful of his Welsh origins, and he completed Owain Glyndwr's work, even though not as Glyndwr would have visualised. But, under him, all England was ruled by a Celtic king.

Hester Lynch Salusbury, 1740–1821

Hester Lynch Salusbury (Mrs Thrale)

Hester Salusbury was a woman of outstanding charm, wit and intelligence. She is remembered because, as Mrs. Thrale, she was for twenty years the friend and confidante of the great Dr. Johnson, but her lively turn of phrase and the originality of her letters and diaries prove her to have been a personality in her own right.

The Salusburys were a Caernarvonshire family, and her mother, a wealthy young woman, married her own cousin, John Salusbury of Bachygraig. He was an extravagant man—Hester appears to have taken after her father in this respect—and spent both his own and his wife's money freely, with the result that his house had to be let and the young couple took refuge in a nearby cottage. Here they remained for several years, until John's mother died, leaving him sufficient money to restore his fortunes. In this cottage, Hester was born—the only one of their six children to survive infancy.

She was an attractive little girl, with fair curls and blue eyes, and both her parents were inordinately proud of her. Because of this, she was spoiled and somewhat precocious. This was before the Victorian era, and children were far from being 'seen but not heard'. One of Hester's earliest memories was of being taken to the theatre by her father's friends, the Duke and Duchess of Leeds, and afterwards going backstage to meet Mr. Quinn, the leading actor, who made much of her and taught her to recite Satan's speech to the sun from *Paradise Lost*. This she declaimed, with great dramatic fervour, at six years of age.

Another adult who indulged her and gave her presents was her uncle, Sir Robert Salusbury-Cotton, who nicknamed her 'Fiddle' and frequently referred to his intention of leaving her £10,000. But he died suddenly without making a will, and his niece had nothing.

His heir was his brother, Sir Thomas Lynch Salusbury-Cotton, the owner of Offley Place. The Salusburys were on good terms with him and visited him frequently, staying in the Dower House at Offley. During one of these visits, when Hester was twenty-one years of age, her uncle announced, half seriously, half in jest, that he intended to introduce to her a wealthy suitor. He had met in the village, he said, 'an excellent, incomparable young man', who had come to see the place where his father had been born. The young man was rich; his father, a self-made man, had left him a fortune. His name was Thrale and he was the owner of a large brewery in London. His arrival at Offley caused a storm in the Salusbury family which ended in tragedy.

Sir Thomas Salusbury encouraged him, and Mrs. Salusbury liked him, but Hester and her father, for different reasons, detested him. Hester found him stiff and ungracious; John Salusbury was horrified at the very idea of his daughter marrying a brewer. Thrale was attracted to the vivacious, proud girl, whose conversational sallies left his slower mind far behind hers; moreover, he was dazzled at the prospect of marriage with Sir Thomas Salusbury's niece. He went out of his way to meet her, paying frequent calls at the Dower House and at Offley Place. Her father became so angry that he accused her of encouraging him. Hester hotly denied this, stating roundly that she had no wish ever to see Thrale again, let alone marry him. But her father did not believe her, and a wretched argument followed, which lasted until the early hours of the morning.

At nine o'clock, John Salusbury walked across the Park to see Sir Thomas, probably with the intention of asking him to discourage Thrale's attentions. Exactly what happened during that interview is not known, but before mid-day John Salusbury was carried back to the Dower House, dead. He had had a heart attack.

He was not a rich man. The family home in Wales, Bachygraig, was left to his wife, but there was scarcely enough money to keep it in a reasonable state of repair, let alone to live in it. To Hester he left £5,000, which sum was doubled by her uncle—possibly as an inducement to marry Thrale, whom he regarded as an ideal match. The girl, who believed herself to be unprepossessing and lacking in talent, gave way to the force of circumstances and accepted the brewer as soon as the period of mourning for her father was over. As she somewhat quaintly records in her personal diary: 'He deigned to accept my undesired hand'.

Hester had always kept a diary, and continued to do so, at intermittent intervals, throughout her married life. It filled a collection of note-books, and was confined not only to accounts of day-to-day household matters, but also contained her comments and descriptions of people and events. It was later published, under the title *Thraliana*, and reveals her as a shrewd observer with a sense of humour and a certain amount of self-mockery. Here is her dispassionate sketch of her husband:

He was indeed much kinder than I had counted on to a plain girl, who had not one attraction in his eyes. . . . With regard to his wife, he is little tender of her person though very partial of her understanding, but he is obliging to nobody and confers a favour less pleasingly than many a man refuses to confer one. Mr. Thrale's person is manly, his countenance agreeable, his eyes steady and of the

Bachygraig, the Salusbury family home in Wales

deepest blue, his look neither soft nor severe, neither sprightly nor gloomy, but thoughtful and intelligent. He is a man wholly, as I think, out of the power of mimicry. He loves money and is diligent to obtain it, but he loves liberality too and is willing enough both to give generously and to spend fashionably. It must, I think, be something more than common that can affect him strongly, either with hope, fear, anger, love, or joy.

Thirteen years later, she comments:

The easiness of his temper and slowness to take offence add greatly to his value as a domestic man, yet I think his servants do not love him, and I am not sure that his children have much affection for him.

As a matter of fact, his daughters were very fond of their father, and although he and Hester were quite incompatible in temperament—she resented his reserve, he despised her apparently superficial preoccupation with social matters—the marriage was a successful one, each developing a respect for the good qualities of the other. Thrale recognised that his wife had a good business head and was an extremely practical woman. He confided in her when he ran into financial problems, and she gave him good advice about the financial side of running the brewery. He grew to admire her many talents, and eventually encouraged her when she began to entertain the literary figures of the day. She was well-read, and could translate Latin, French and Italian into sound, idiomatic English. He was content to remain a stolid, silent figure, listening without comment to the witty conversation that went on in his wife's salon. She, on her part, came to value her husband's solid reliability. She was flattered when he commissioned Sir Joshua

Reynolds to paint her portrait, but not pleased with the result, criticising it in a light, epigrammatic couplet:

> In these features so placid, so cold, so serene,
> What trace of the wit or the Welshwoman's seen?

It is interesting to notice that several years spent in fashionable London society had not erased from her mind a consciousness of her nationality.

Hester Thrale first met the great Dr. Johnson in 1764, when she was a young matron of twenty-four and he, at fifty-five, one of the dominating figures of London's literary world. Oddly enough, it was the unimaginative brewer who first invited Johnson to Streatham Place, the Thrales' new home just outside the city, to the south of Tooting Bec Common. Streatham Place was a large, luxurious, white house, set in parkland, with well-stocked kitchen gardens and glasshouses filled with fruit. No wonder Johnson enjoyed his visits, which soon became very regular, for it was the Thrales' habit to invite him to dinner every Thursday. In 1776, he became for a time a permanent resident. He had a long illness, which left him very depressed. Mr. and Mrs. Thrale, calling to enquire after their friend, were shocked at his condition and insisted on taking him back with them to Streatham, where he remained for the next three months.

Hester nursed him with great devotion, though he must have been a trying patient, for she found him 'greedy, untidy, and not particularly clean'. His chief trouble was insomnia, coupled with a horror of being left alone. Often she would sit up until four in the morning, making him cups of tea (he drank at least sixteen cups every day, usually more), listening to his outbursts of self-pity, and quietly assuring him that she would not leave him until he was ready to go to sleep. As his health improved, he was given complete freedom of the house and gardens. He had his particular chair by the fireside, the library became his own domain and a small summer-house was built in the park so that on fine days he could work outside without interruption. Mr. Thrale even had a small room fitted out to serve as a laboratory, but this had to be abandoned when his guest, working with more enthusiasm than finesse, almost succeeded in blowing up the house.

Hester's mother was also a resident of Streatham Place at this time and she and Dr. Johnson began their acquaintance on a very bad footing. Mrs. Salusbury loved the political and foreign news items in the press, which she would read aloud and comment upon with relish. Johnson detested this habit, and tried to break her of it by inventing completely fictitious 'news' which she would solemnly consider. It took her some time to forgive him for befooling her, but eventually she and the Doctor became good friends.

After his recovery, a room was always kept for Johnson at Streatham, and he kept up his regular weekly visits for sixteen years, arriving on Thursdays and staying until Saturday morning. The Thrales also had a town house and one at fashionable Brighton, and in both Johnson was a welcome guest. He was not the only literary figure to benefit from Hester's interest. Another guest was Fanny Burney, on whom she lavished great kindness, taking her to balls and to the theatre and generally smoothing her pathway into London society. But success went to Fanny's head, for Hester later complained that she became ungrateful and insolent towards her, adding, with characteristic tolerance, 'she is a saucy-spirited little puss, but still I love her dearly for all that.'

Fanny, in her turn, has left us a description of Mrs. Thrale at this period. 'She is a pretty woman still,' she wrote, 'though she has some defect in the mouth which looks like a cut or scar. Her nose is very handsome and complexion very fair, her eyes blue and lustrous.'

It has been suggested that Hester's kindness to Johnson had an entirely selfish motive—the personal celebrity which she would win as a result of his constant presence in her house. But the Doctor himself benefited considerably from his friendship with the Thrales. Not only did they provide for him a dignified background at Streatham; they took him with them when they travelled. He accompanied them to Wales, Bath, Brighton, and France. Indeed, a trip to Florence was arranged, but was never undertaken, as the Thrales' young son died suddenly at the age of ten, just a week prior to the date arranged for their departure. There are no details of this tragedy, apart from a notice published at the time, which states baldly: 'He died suddenly, before his father's door.' Johnson, who hurried to London from Lichfield when he heard the news, was shocked to find the carriage waiting outside the house, to take Mrs. Thrale to Bath. He did not realise that she could not bear to remain in town during the funeral and the period of mourning immediately following it, although she herself notes that, as soon as possible, she had to put away her own grief in order to comfort her husband.

The loss of his only son was a bitter blow to him, although—despite his wife's summary of his character—he was an affectionate father to his daughters. Johnson noted in his diary during a visit to Hester's Welsh property: 'Queeny's goats—149, I think'. Apparently the short-sighted brewer was unable to distinguish all the goats browsing on the slopes of Snowdon and had promised to pay the little girl one penny for every one she pointed out to him; Johnson was her accountant.

Johnson admired the rugged grandeur of Snowdonia, and one of his letters, praising its beauty, was published in Boswell's *Life of*

Samuel Johnson—a portrait by Joshua Reynolds

Johnson. It is interesting that Hester, in the margin of her copy, pencilled, 'Yet to please Mr. Thrale, he feigned abhorrence of it.' Despite years of London life, she remained Welsh at heart and resented her companions' indifference to her native land.

In 1770, Thrale had an attack of apoplexy. He recovered, and lived for almost ten years longer, but was moody and irascible, and the management of the brewery fell to Hester. This she tackled competently, although the task was made difficult by her awe of her husband and his insistence in interfering with her plans. Once, when Johnson, who understood the situation, advised her to tear up a letter of his about some foolish scheme, she noted: 'God knows I durst as well encounter death as disturb Mr. Thrale's letters, or his building plans.'

Towards the end of his life, Thrale became exceedingly stubborn. His doctors had advised him to eat sparingly and to lead a very quiet life, but not only did he eat the very dishes against which he had been warned, he filled the house with company and toyed with the idea of standing as a candidate at the next general election. But, in 1779, he had another seizure and died while Johnson was a guest in the house, leaving a widow of thirty-eight and two young daughters.

After his death, Hester let Streatham Place and moved to Argyll Street, in London, where she continued to entertain Johnson as before. But her old friend was becoming infirm and very trying. He used her house as if it were his own, lying in bed until mid-day and expecting his hostess to prepare his meals herself and to wait on him hand and foot. He scolded her for extravagance and was rude to her other guests, but she continued to bear with him because she felt sorry for him. In 1783 he was still a constant visitor, and it was at this time that a new interest came into Hester's life.

Her daughters were taking music lessons from an Italian master, Gabriel Piozzi, a man of about her own age, poor, but considerate and charming. Hester found herself strongly attracted to him but, according to the rigid code of the eighteenth century, he was so much her social inferior as to make marriage with him out of the question. It may well be that Johnson suspected the way her thoughts were turning, for Boswell gives an account of a conversation at Argyll Street concerning a young lady who had 'married beneath her'. Mrs. Thrale was all for mildness and conciliation, but her ageing mentor pontificated:

Madam, we must distinguish. Were I a man of rank, I would not let a daughter starve who had made a mean marriage. But having voluntarily degraded herself from the station to which she was originally entitled, I would support her only in that rank which she had chosen, and not attempt to put her on a level with my other daughters. You are to consider, Madam, that it is our duty to maintain the subordination of civilised society, and gross and shameful deviation from rank should be punished.

This stratification of society was taken for granted at the time; it is reflected in the novels of both Fanny Burney and Jane Austen. So the worldly-wise Mrs. Thrale must have realised exactly what would happen when, in 1784, she announced that she intended to marry Piozzi.

She herself had no pretensions to grandeur; the widow of a wealthy brewer, she proposed to become the wife of a poor music master, but her former friends took a very different view. Many of them, including Fanny Burney, dropped her after expressing shocked surprise. Her two daughters became estranged from her and were never really reconciled to the match. As for Johnson, he sent her a vituperative letter, accusing her of making an 'ignominious marriage', abandoning her children and her religion, and begging her to change her mind before it was too late. But too late it was, and she replied with spirit, pointing out that her second husband's rank was in no way inferior to that of Thrale, and accusing Johnson of meanness in considering lack of fortune to be a disgrace. She reminded the Doctor of their long friendship, but stated categorically that, until he changed his opinion of Piozzi, she would not meet him again. The quarrel went on for several months, although a friendly correspondence was resumed shortly before Johnson's death.

Piozzi was no fortune-hunter, and Hester found great happiness with her second husband. He was handsome, gentle and unaffected, with a sincere admiration for his wife's talents. He had complete control of her money, but managed it well, with genuine concern for her best interests. He also encouraged her to publish some of her writing, and in 1786, after Johnson's death, her *Anecdotes of Johnson* appeared, to be followed by *Letters To and From Johnson* and an account of her travels in Italy.

Her style was not appreciated by readers of her generation, for she wrote as she talked, in an era when mannered and stately prose was the accepted mode, and her other books—one on history and one on English usage—met with scant success. But to the modern reader her private journals—published as *Thraliana* in 1942—give a true picture of a vivid personality.

Not long after their marriage, Mr. and Mrs. Piozzi left London for North Wales, where Piozzi designed and had built a new house, 'Brynbella'. To please her, he also had her family home, Bachygraig, 'set up, . . . to please his silly wife, and gilded the Llewenyi lion on its top.'

After her daughters were married, Hester eagerly agreed to the adoption of an orphaned nephew of her husband. He was brought up at 'Brynbella', and took the name of John Salusbury. Eventually he inherited Hester's property, for her daughters had been well provided for by their father. He was knighted, and became Sheriff of his county, but he never forgot her kindness and his attitude towards her was always that of a true son.

In 1809, Gabriel Piozzi died at Brynbella, of gout, having given Hester fifteen years of complete happiness. She never regretted her second marriage, but five years later, young John Salusbury being of age, she gave him the house in Wales which was so full of memories and retired to Bath, where she took 'a pretty, neat house and decent establishment for a widowed lady, and shall exist a true "Bath Cat" for the remainder of my life.' She continued, however, to take a lively interest in everything that went on around her, contemplating events with a philosophical detachment.

On her eightieth birthday, she attended a concert, followed by a ball at which she led the dancing, partnered by her nephew. Moreover, she still danced with grace and dignity, and a sense of restraint which prevented her from appearing a figure of fun. She remained sweet-tempered to the end of her life, showing no inclination at all to interfere in the concerns of Sir John's family or those of her daughters. But this was to be her last ball. Early in the following year she died 'in the trust and fear of God'. She had been a remarkable woman, meeting everyone on equal terms and always ready to give help, for she was quite free from jealousy in a particularly jealous era. An extract from her diary sums up her character: 'It has always been my maxim never to influence the inclination of another. Let me endeavour to please God, and to have only my own faults and follies, not those of another, to answer for.'

A charming and truly disinterested woman, Hester deserved the happiness of her later years.

Sarah Siddons, 1755–1831

Sarah Siddons

In the middle years of the eighteenth century, the place of the actor in society was undergoing a gradual change. There were still many companies which toured, and they still, on occasion, had to perform in a local barn, but the play was the chief source of entertainment at the time, and most provincial towns had a theatre. In London and other cities, leading actors and actresses were frequently the guests of the aristocracy; in short, the stage was becoming respectable.

The better touring companies were often family affairs, in which the parents, children and a few young actors and actresses who were learning their trade and travelled under the supervision of the principals, were all involved. Some still went about on foot, lugging their properties on handcarts. The more affluent would own or hire a coach and horses.

Such a company was Roger Kemble's, which was well-known in Wales and the Border counties. Kemble himself had started his career as a barber, and took to acting because he was good-looking and had a flair for it. His wife came of a theatrical family, the Wards, but her father had not wanted her to act and disapproved of the marriage to Kemble, whom he disliked. Kemble himself claimed descent from the Kembles of Pembridge Castle and instilled into his family a pride in the martyred priest, John Kemble, who was revered both in Hereford and in Monmouth. He was himself a Catholic, but his wife was not; however, they came to an amicable agreement by which their male children were to be brought up

Sarah spent her early years on tour with her parents' company, and probably was carried on stage before she was old enough to walk. It was the custom at that time, when a touring company arrived at a small town, that they marched in procession through the streets, preceded by a man who beat upon a drum to announce their arrival. Sometimes, one of the children of the company was trained to balance the drum upon its head; tradition has it that Sarah was, for a time, the girl who carried the drum, and that it was to this that she owed her wonderful carriage and walk in later years. Certainly she was brought up in an atmosphere of theatre.

Mr. and Mrs. Kemble, like many another actor and actress, were determined that their children should not adopt the stage as a profession. It was quite in order for them to appear in small parts when they were little, but as they grew older and the company prospered the children were sent away to school, Sarah and her sisters to Worcester, which their parents visited frequently as a part of their circuit, John Philip and his brother to the Catholic Seminary at Sedgely Park.

Sarah profited by the years she spent at Thornlea House School, although she was not happy there at first. All her life she was, when not on the stage, a fundamentally shy person, and her fellow-pupils thought her proud. But they were impressed by her knowledge of Milton and Shakespeare; her vocabulary was tremendous, and she wrote fluently and spelled accurately, at a period when many society women could do neither. Sometimes, when the company happened to be in the vicinity, the children were taken from school for a time to appear in a play. Before her formal education was completed Sarah had taken the parts of the boy king in *Richard III*, Ariel in *The Tempest*, and been cast in contemporary drama also. She never dreamed of being anything but an actress, and at fifteen

The Siddons house in Upper Baker Street

in his faith and the girls in hers.

They were touring in Wales when their first child, a daughter, was born. Mrs. Kemble actually appeared in a play on the day previous to the birth, and on 5 July 1755, the local midwife of Brecon was hastily summoned to the Shoulder of Mutton Inn, where the Kembles had put up, and delivered the baby, who, a few days later, was baptised Sarah at St. Mary's Church. Mrs. Kemble recovered quickly, and the tour continued, as it did after the birth of other children, for the Kembles had several, of whom two, Sarah and John Philip, were destined to become famous.

left school and became, officially, a member of her father's company.

In 1770 the Kembles were once more at Brecon, and here they realised that their eldest child was rapidly developing into a woman. A local man, Mr. Evans, who owned a small estate, fell in love with her and asked her father's permission to approach her as a suitor. The Kembles were pleased, although they considered their daughter too young for marriage. Evans was rich; he would take the girl away from the stage. They were prepared to encourage him and told Sarah to do so.

The girl, however, had other ideas. She had fallen in love with a young man in the company, William Siddons. William was not a very good actor, but he was both handsome and kind; promises had been exchanged between the young couple, and Sarah, with the determination which was to be hers all of her life, declared flatly that she would marry him and no-one else.

Her father was furious. Not only had Siddons been paying court to his daughter without seeking his permission; Sarah was proposing to marry an actor and so tie herself irrevocably to the profession. And she had only just had her fifteenth birthday; her parents had not foreseen such precocity—though why they had not, in the atmosphere in which they lived, it is hard to imagine.

It was decided to part the pair. William was dismissed, Sarah was to be sent away. But Roger Kemble was a fair-minded man. When an actor left a company, it was customary for him to have a Benefit Night, from which he received the proceeds. William Siddons' Benefit took place at Brecon, where it attracted a great deal of attention, for, unknown to the family, people had been following the affair with avid interest. A local man was involved, and, moreover, they regarded the beautiful Miss Kemble as one of themselves, since she had been born in the town.

Taking advantage of this sympathy, William included in his final address the entire sad story, told in his own very poor verse and blaming the Kembles. The poem—if poem it can be called—began:

Ye ladies of Brecon, whose hearts ever feel
For wrongs like this I'm about to reveal,
Excuse the first product, nor pass unregarded
The plaints of poor Colin, a lover discarded.

There was much more in the same strain, and Mr. and Mrs. Kemble, who always believed that their public life was one thing and their private life another, objected strongly to having personal concerns paraded in this way. They did, however, relent sufficiently to agree that Sarah and William might write to one another, believing that their daughter would soon outgrow her romantic ideal.

A situation had been found for Sarah as a lady's maid to Lady Mary Greatheed, of Guy's Cliffe, Warwick, at a salary of £10.00 a year. She had no wish to go, but Lady Mary, who was the daughter of the Duke of Ancaster, treated her very kindly and before long she became more of a companion than a maid, dining with the family when they had guests and attending social functions in Lady Mary's company. In later years, when she was to be an honoured guest in great houses in London and in Bath, this training stood her in good stead. The 'Divine Sarah' was never at a loss in society.

While she was at Guy's Cliffe Sarah met David Garrick, and plucked up courage to ask him for an audition. He was impressed by her outstanding beauty, but not by her acting ability, so nothing came of it. Some years later, she did appear with Garrick, but did not do well. He appears to have had an inhibiting effect upon her.

She continued to write to William regularly, and when she was eighteen persuaded her parents to let her return to them. Her determination must have convinced them, for not only did they agree that she could become an actress, they allowed her to marry William and took him back into the company. William and Sarah were married in Holy Trinity Church, Coventry, in 1773, and spent the next year on the Kemble circuit.

In 1775, in order to gain more experience, Sarah and William Siddons, now the parents of a boy, joined Mr. Younger's company. Younger, of course, worked a different circuit and the tour took them south, to Devizes. Here they put up at the Bear Inn, where the landlord was a man named Lawrence.

One evening, before she went to the theatre, Sarah was sitting in one of the rooms of the inn when the landlord's little boy, a child of six, came running in. He stared at Sarah for a few minutes, then fetched paper and crayons and announced that he would draw her portrait. Naturally, she expected the usual childish scrawl, but to her astonishment was presented with an extraordinarily good likeness. Lawrence told her that little Tom had always possessed an amazing gift for drawing, and Sarah agreed. Their paths were destined to cross again, years afterwards, when Thomas Lawrence, by that time a famous Academician and Court Painter, was to cause great unhappiness in the Siddons family.

The following year, while playing at Cheltenham, Sarah's performance attracted the notice of Mr. Bate, a friend of Garrick. He wrote of her in glowing terms, urging Garrick to engage this brilliant young actress, who was certainly destined for fame. Garrick agreed and, when her contract with Mr. Younger came to an end, she was offered the chance to make her London debut at Drury Lane. Loyally, she insisted that William should also be engaged, and this was agreed upon. William was well aware of the fact that his wife had far more talent than he did; he was content with small parts, and

later left the stage altogether and became Sarah's business manager.

At that period it was usual for a player of standing to provide his own wardrobe—at least, the bulk of it—and anyone of the eminence of Garrick, Sheridan or 'Perdita' Robinson would possess a sumptuous collection of costumes and wigs. Sarah Siddons had nothing sufficiently magnificent for Drury Lane, so she appeared in her first part, as Portia in *The Merchant of Venice*, dressed in somewhat shabby clothes provided by the management. She did not do well. She was terrified by Garrick, and by the size of the theatre, which, compared with the provincial ones to which she was accustomed, was huge. She never in all her life forgot her lines, but on this occasion, from sheer fright, she became inaudible.

Some of the actresses were inimical to the newcomer, and the critics were scathing. She did better as Lady Anne in 'Richard III', but then Garrick put on an unpopular play by a contemporary author and the audience expressed their disapproval with hissing and cat-calls. Sarah was led to believe that the fault was hers. Garrick did not renew the Siddons' contract at the end of the season and she returned, humiliated, to the provincial circuits, where she became increasingly popular.

In 1778 Sarah was engaged by Mr. Palmer, of the Theatre Royal, Bath, to play there and also at his theatre in Bristol. The travelling was gruelling, but Sarah, throughout her life, was fortunate in having very good health and it did mean that the Siddons family could have a permanent home in Bath. There were two children now, a boy named Henry and a girl, Sally, who was always her mother's best-loved child. John Philip Kemble was by now becoming known as an actor (Roger Kemble's intention not to allow his children to go on the stage proved a failure) and he sometimes appeared with his sister. Bath was a fashionable watering place. She became well-known, especially as a tragedienne, and stayed with Palmer for four years, during which time her third child, Maria, was born. Then, the miracle happened; she was invited to go back to Drury Lane, as a leading member of the company.

David Garrick had retired, and Richard Brinsley Sheridan now managed Drury Lane. It was his father who saw her at Bath and urged his son to employ her. At first, she hesitated. She loved Bath, and her memories of Drury Lane were unpleasant ones. But the Sheridans were so persuasive, the salary they offered so tempting, that she agreed. At the end of her farewell performance at Bath, she took her three children onto the stage with her while she made her final speech, putting them forward as her reason for accepting the Sheridans' offer.

Her second reception in London was very different from her first. She appeared in Garrick's version of *The Fatal Marriage*, a play which, though now completely forgotten, gave an actress well-versed in tragic roles an opportunity to give rein to the full gamut of emotion. Next day, she was the talk of the town. Her little son, Henry, appeared as her child, audiences were touched, and the critics acclaimed her ability in the demanding role of Isabella. In a remarkably short time, Mrs. Siddons was established in London, and she never lost her pre-eminence.

She appeared in Shakespeare—Lady Macbeth was her most celebrated role—and also in contemporary drama. One of her most significant successes was as Mrs. Haller in *The Stranger*, a translation of a German play. This script is little known now, but it was the precursor of a much-exploited theme of modern drama—the wife who deserts her husband, only to return to him for the sake of love and family ties. Mrs. Haller, who leaves husband and family for 'the

Mrs Siddons in the character of Lady Macbeth

Stranger', only to be forgiven in the end, was the original of Paula Tanqueray, and a host of other misguided heroines. Mrs. Haller's husband forgave her; Paula killed herself. Eighteenth century audiences did not easily accept the reinstatement of an erring wife, and some identified the actress with her role. But the play attracted tremendous publicity, and whenever Mrs. Siddons appeared, she was acclaimed. She was even appointed as Preceptress in English Reading to the Royal Princesses, and was invited to Buckingham House. Here she was somewhat disconcerted by the Princess Amelia, then aged three, who when her new tutor bent to embrace her, extended a chubby hand to be kissed. But Sarah was always popular with George III and his family, and gave many readings to the Royal circle.

Sometimes she went on tour, and on occasion visited Ireland, where she appeared in Dublin and other cities, but she was never popular there. It was in Ireland that she made the acquaintance of the Galindos, husband and wife, who were later to do her so much harm. She enjoyed the journey to Holyhead, but her first sea crossing caused her great discomfort, and she wrote to a friend:

> I was dreadfully sick, and so were my poor sister and Mrs. Brereton. Mr. Siddons was pretty well; and here, my dear friends, let me give you a little wholesome advice; allways (you see I have forgot to spell) go to bed the instant you go on board, for by lying horizontally, and keeping very quiet, you can cheat the sea of half its influence.

By 1790, the Siddons had a town house in the Strand. Sally and Maria were at school in France, and the theatre-going public—and that meant all the intelligentsia of London—was at Sarah Siddons' feet. William Siddons had left the stage to become her manager, and it is worth noting that, in these years before the passing of The Married Women's Property Act, all she earned belonged, in law, to him. Neither seems to have resented it: there was never any breath of disagreement between the couple. Sarah was the acknowledged breadwinner, William accepted a secondary role. In return, she never resented his control over her earnings, and he never misused his power.

It was at this point that Thomas Lawrence re-entered Sarah's life. They met, occasionally, at Buckingham House, for he was by now Court Painter, and he made several studies of Sarah, as did Reynolds and Gainsborough, the other leading artists of the day. He was invited to the house in the Strand, and, when Sally and Maria were brought home from their French School in 1793, became a constant visitor. He wanted to become the suitor of the elder daughter, Sally, and confided his hopes in Sarah. She did not disapprove, but remembering her own courtship, told him that as Sally was barely eighteen there could be no official engagement as yet. But she was fond of Lawrence and the marriage was to her liking. She encouraged his visits and Sally became very attached to him. Within the family circle, their engagement was a fait accompli.

Maria Siddons, aged fifteen, had all her mother's precocity. She was a very beautiful girl, with thick black hair, dark eyes, and rosy cheeks which appeared to glow with the bloom of health and youth but, had anyone been aware of the fact, in reality signalled the consumption from which she died. She, too, was attracted by the young artist, and deliberately set out to win him from her more retiring sister. Before long, Lawrence had transferred his affections from Sally to Maria.

Sally Siddons must have been one of the most generous girls in the world. Once convinced that Lawrence and Maria truly loved one another, she quietly effaced herself and let the courtship proceed. Maria, however, was still very immature and enjoyed a romantic situation. She stole out, thinly clad, in the fogs of a London winter, to clandestine meetings with Lawrence. She caught cold after cold, and became really ill. The situation went on for some time because both parents were too busy to notice what was happening, but, when the state of Maria's health began to cause alarm, her mother got the story out of her.

At first, Sarah was furious at Lawrence's behaviour, and forbade him the house. Maria grew worse; Sally was thin and pale. Eventually William Siddons summoned the young man and gave official sanction to his engagement to Maria. A dowry was agreed upon, and Lawrence once more came frequently to the Siddons' home.

Little can be said to excuse his behaviour, except that he was a great artist, and had all an artist's ability to ignore the suffering he caused to others. Now that he was the acknowledged suitor of Maria, he once again became attracted to Sally, telling her that it was she whom he truly loved. Sarah, once in possession of the facts, decided that a little separation would be good for all parties. She packed Maria off to an old friend of hers in Clifton, Mrs. Pennington. Sally, she took with her on tour.

Lawrence's behaviour was despicable. He continued to write to both girls, and, with Mrs. Pennington's contrivance, visited Maria at Clifton. But Maria was now very ill. Her hectic beauty, her vivacity, her restlessness, were all symptoms of consumption. William, who had gout, had gone to Bath in search of a cure when Mrs. Pennington wrote to Sarah, telling her that she was very disturbed about Maria's health. Sarah sent Sally to care for her sister, promising to come herself as soon as her tour was over.

Before she went, she saw Lawrence and told him in no uncertain terms her opinion of his conduct. Lawrence was contrite, but protested that it was Sally, and only Sally, that he loved. Sarah reached Clifton in a very uneasy frame of mind.

There she found Maria much worse—dying, in fact. But the young girl had all her mother's sense of the dramatic and, fully aware of her condition, summoned Sarah and Sally to her bedside one afternoon. Here, she said to her sister: 'Promise me, Sally, never to be the wife of Mr. Lawrence. I cannot bear to think of your being so.' Sally, who still loved Lawrence, tried to avoid giving the promise. 'Dearest Maria, think of nothing that agitates you,' she replied. But Maria was insistent. She made Sally, her mother, and Mrs. Pennington clasp her hands, and wrung from Sally a promise that she would never become Lawrence's wife. Soon afterwards she died, and was buried at Clifton.

Sally returned to London, where Lawrence soon began haunting the house, though he was never invited inside. Her father was with her, her mother at the theatre. One Sunday, the artist waylaid the family as they left church, with such extravagant protestations of his love for Sally that sensible William Siddons was quite sure he was mentally deranged. Soon afterwards, Sally wrote to him, finally dismissing him from her life.

Sarah crossed once more to Ireland, where she again met with a hostile reception and encountered other difficulties of her own making. She had befriended a couple named Galindo. The wife was an actress, the husband a fencing-master. They were neither well-off nor successful, so with characteristic generosity Sarah hired their carriage and took fencing lessons from Mr. Galindo. The fact that he chose to adore her, to sit at her feet, she ignored. Such extravagant emotions were quite common in the theatrical world, and Sarah, nearly fifty and growing stout, simply did not consider that there might be trouble ahead.

Sally was not well that year. She had always been asthmatic, and her condition worsened. In March, 1803, William wrote to Sarah urging her to return, as their daughter was gravely ill. Her crossing was delayed by storms; eventually she arrived at Holyhead and travelled by stage-coach to Shrewsbury, en route for London. But here a letter from her husband reached her. There was no need to hurry. Sally was dead.

The loss of this child, her dearest, affected Sarah for months, but she was too much of an artiste to allow anything to separate her for long from her career. Her brother, John Philip Kemble, had recently opened a new theatre in Covent Garden. She broke with Sheridan and, after a holiday on the Welsh border, where they re-visited their childhood haunts, she joined her brother's Company. But the new theatre was burned down and had to be rebuilt. In 1808, William died, and when the brother and sister re-opened at Covent Garden John felt that, as the reconstruction of the theatre had proved so expensive, he must increase the prices of admission. This caused riots; the audiences constantly interrupted actors with shrieks of 'O.P.! O.P.!' and eventually he was obliged to compromise and restore the original prices of the cheaper seats.

Then the Galindos came to London, anticipating that Sarah would use her influence to get them work in the theatre. But they were not very good, and she could give little help. Mrs. Galindo published a resentful and spiteful 'open letter', in which she accused Sarah of betraying their friendship and alienating her husband's affections. The accusation was patently untrue, but some people believed it, and Sarah's friends urged her to prosecute the Galindos. This she refused to do, observing dispassionately that it would do her no good, and cause great harm to the Galindos' young children.

After this, she withdrew gradually from public life, making her last stage appearance in 1812, as Lady Macbeth. She lived on, in semi-retirement, for a further nineteen years, giving occasional private performances and readings. She lived to see the death of the detested Thomas Lawrence in 1830, and was probably glad that she had become reconciled to him in old age, although he was

never again received in her house. And, in 1829, she was present to watch her brilliant niece, Fanny Kemble, appear as Juliet. Through Fanny, the stage tradition was handed on. Sarah herself died in 1831, and was buried in Paddington Cemetery.

Rupert, the great-great-grandson of Sarah Siddons, by her statue in Paddington Green. When the statue was unveiled by Sir Henry Irving in 1897, it was the first outdoor statue to a woman in London, apart from members of the Royal Family

Robert Owen, 1771–1858

Robert Owen

Robert Owen is frequently spoken of as 'the father of Socialism' and the direct forerunner of Marxist doctrines. In some ways this is true; in others, a distortion. He was more of a sociologist than a socialist, and, unlike Marx, had no interest in political movements. Brought up during the Industrial Revolution, he saw the evils which followed it and felt the exploitation of labour to be morally unjustifiable. He sought to improve conditions, not by revolution, but by a gradual programme of education. His theories were new and attracted hostility from fellow employers who regarded him as a dangerous crank. He managed to justify himself many times, and became a very wealthy man, well able to afford the money he spent so lavishly on the welfare of his employees, but he remained a paternalist and it is doubtful if he ever considered his workers to be his social or intellectual equals.

Owen was born at Newtown, in Montgomeryshire, the son of a saddler who was also the village postmaster. He was a very intelligent child, and by the time he was seven was reading any books that came his way. Three ladies of the neighbourhood, all strong adherents to Methodism, took an interest in him, and lent him books, many of a religious content. Owen discarded all orthodox creeds, but nevertheless remained a deeply religious man to the end of his life. His schoolmaster, Mr. Thickness, was impressed by his precocious pupil, and before he was nine most of the boy's time at school was spent in teaching others. His parents encouraged him to think for himself and to form his own judgments.

He appears to have remained unspoiled and even docile, recalling in his autobiography that his father only thrashed him once, when he had refused point-blank to carry out some request of his mother's. After the punishment, he was told that he must now obey his mother. 'At length I said, quietly and firmly, "You may kill me, but I will not do it", and this decided the contest. There was no attempt ever afterwards to correct me; but this difference was soon made up on both sides, and I continued to be the favourite I had always been.'

Before his tenth birthday, Owen left school and started work in a draper's shop in Newtown. He remained there for a year, then went to London, where his eldest brother had a shop. His brother arranged for him to be apprenticed to Mr. McGuffog, a haberdasher of Stamford, in whose house he was to live for three years. From that time Owen became completely self-supporting, and never again asked his parents for any financial help.

Mr. McGuffog proved to be a very good employer who treated Owen well, but at the end of three years the boy left him and returned to London, where he found work as an assistant in a large drapery store where the owners were out to make as much profit as possible. The shop opened at 8 a.m. and shut at 10 p.m.—often half-past; after this, the counters had to be tidied and the display arranged for the following day. Owen later noted: 'Frequently at two o'clock in the morning . . . I have scarcely been able, with the aid of the bannisters to go upstairs to bed. And thus I had about five hours for sleep.'

Eventually Owen moved to Manchester and by the time he was eighteen had become part owner of a small factory. He prospered, eventually becoming a partner in the flourishing Chorlton Twist Company. At twenty-seven, he was a well-known figure in Manchester, and many of his business associates confidently predicted that he would soon become one of the richest businessmen in Lancashire. Among his friends he numbered John Dalton, the mathematician, and Samuel Taylor Coleridge, the poet.

He was not, however, to remain in Manchester. A journey to Glasgow in search of business contacts brought about an introduction to David Dale, a banker and religious leader, the owner of the big cotton mills at New Lanark. Owen was interested in New Lanark. At that time, labour was not too easily obtained in Scotland; the lowland farms still attracted the majority of workers. It was possible to recruit families from the Highlands, where prospects were poor, and also the local Parish Guardians were only too ready to supply 'parish apprentices' in large numbers—pauper children whom they wanted to get off their hands. Such workers, however, had to be housed, and Mr. Dale had erected several one-storey houses for them in the area surrounding the mills. A man of strong religious principles, he did his best according to his limited vision, and his best was certainly better than the slums of Manchester could provide. Owen, who had for years been concerned about the overcrowding and bad living conditions of factory workers, felt that New Lanark was at least a purpose-built environment, capable of improvement according to his own ideas.

There was another attraction in Scotland. Owen had several times met David Dale's daughter, Caroline-Anne, and a strong liking had grown between them. He asked her father's permission to marry her, but Dale, disliking Owen whom he considered an opportunist, would not hear of it. Owen returned to Manchester, but was soon back again in Glasgow armed with the backing of his partners in a proposal that the Chorlton Twist Company should buy New Lanark, which he knew Mr. Dale wished to sell. Dale was dubious at first; he felt Owen was too young to be a responsible owner. But Chorlton Twist did buy New Lanark, and soon afterwards Mr. Dale withdrew his objections to Caroline-Anne's choice of a husband. The couple were married in January 1800, and Owen assumed the position of resident manager at New Lanark.

Owen's work at New Lanark marks him as an educationalist, far in advance of his time. He found that he had to deal with adult labourers, both men and women, who had been driven by poverty to take up factory work, and also with the 'parish apprentices' who were really a source of cheap labour of which he strongly disapproved. He realised, however, that the system could not be reformed at once. First of all, he set to work to improve the living conditions of the adult workers and their families. An additional storey was added to every house, so that the inhabitants could be provided with proper sleeping quarters and, because each family was now treated as an individual unit, an incentive to take pride in the cleanliness and general appearance of themselves and their homes. The 'parish apprentices' he gradually phased out. They

were urged to leave New Lanark on the completion of their indentures, and were not replaced.

This decision appears, on the face of it, very harsh. Owen, however, had a strongly-held theory which he wanted to put into practice, and the 'parish apprentices' were not suitable material for his experiment.

He believed that harmony between workers and employers could be achieved only on a foundation of mutual trust coupled with a common code of social conduct. This, he felt, could be built up by means of a carefully planned educational programme, which had to be started in early childhood. The 'parish apprentices', most of whom came to the mills at the age of ten, were too old for this programme, so he concentrated on the children of his adult employees.

Considering that Owen designed his New Lanark schools five years after the end of the Napoleonic Wars, his ideas on education were wonderfully advanced. He felt the retention of fact to be only part of the process, the aim of which was to develop a child's mind as a whole. He advocated lessons in the open air, nature walks and play; singing

New Lanark, where Owen put his theories as an educationalist and social reformer into practice

and dancing occupied almost as much of the curriculum at New Lanark as the basic reading, writing and arithmetic. Visual aids were important; his teachers used maps, charts, paints and coloured blocks. In 1816 an infant school was opened, where the children 'were not to be annoyed with books, but were to be taught the uses and nature of the common things around them . . . when their curiosity was excited so as to induce them to ask questions respecting them.' Pictures, models, plants and living creatures were there for these young children to handle and to understand. At one point he expressed grave doubts as to the value of any book to a child younger than ten years old.

Ten was the very youngest age at which Owen could consider the employment of children at New Lanark—this in the days before any Factory Acts had been passed—and then they were only permitted to work for part of the day, the other part to be spent in school. His New Lanark schools attracted a great deal of attention, and within a few years Owen was able to demonstrate that his work force made up a happy, thinking community. Labour was never difficult to recruit, and his employees were willing and industrious, so that despite the expense incurred by his methods, his account books always showed a handsome profit.

However, before very long a serious flaw was discovered in Owen's system. He objected to any form of religious teaching in his schools. This was not because he was himself an atheist, or even an agnostic—he was simply against the arbitrary indoctrination of children into any formal creed. Dogmatism, he held, had produced more evil in the world than good. He was prepared to allow his workpeople to practise any form of worship they wished, or none at all, but he was insistent that, once a man's character had been formed, religious freedom was essential.

His contemporaries in the fields of education and philanthropy were men of deep religious convictions; his partners in the New Lanark enterprise were Quakers. Before long, they began to voice objections to his methods. The teaching of music and dancing were suspect, the absence of any doctrinaire instruction was worse. In vain Owen instanced the honesty and sobriety of his New Lanark work force: he was unable to convince his opponents that he was not engaged in training a colony of atheists. Gradually, his partners brought about the introduction of religious teaching in the place of dancing and singing. Eventually, they managed to secure for themselves the control of the schools, and, although the education given to the children of New Lanark continued to be good, Owen's pioneering work was almost forgotten; a century later, when similar schemes were introduced into schools by Maria Montessori, they were hailed as wonderful new educational discoveries.

Owen, however, was not unwilling to leave New Lanark. He was now a wealthy man of considerable public standing. He turned his mind to a plan which he felt would not only relieve the unemployment which followed the Napoleonic War, but would also form the basis of a new order of society. The result of his plan was the Owenite movement, and it is this that stamps him as a pioneer of Socialism. His idea, simplified, was that wages represented a false value; they should be replaced by 'the natural standard of value . . . human labour, or the combined manual and mental powers of men called into action. . . . That which can create new wealth is, of course, worth the wealth which it creates. The producer should have a fair and fixed proportion of the wealth he creates.' This, he felt, could be achieved by the establishment of what he referred to as 'Villages of Co-operation', where agriculture and industry could exist

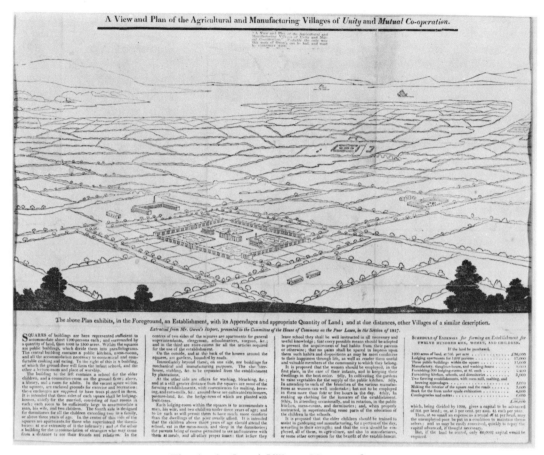

The plan for Owen's Village of Co-operation

side by side, sharing their produce to the benefit of all.

Landowners and factory owners strongly opposed Owen's theory, but it aroused a considerable amount of interest amongst the working classes, and Co-operative Societies sprang up in London and in Brighton, which attempted to raise money for the foundation of Villages of Co-operation. Owen himself, however, was interested in certain religious communities in the United States, which organised themselves on broadly similar lines of thought. In 1824 he visited the Rappite community in Indiana, and, since they were about to move to a new site, he severed his connection with New Lanark and bought the entire Rappite village, which he re-named New Harmony, in order to put his ideas into practice. He advertised New Harmony in lectures on both sides of the Atlantic, in which he stated that he would welcome 'the industrious and well-disposed of all nations' as members of the Co-operative community.

By 1826, Owen was busy drawing up a constitution for the settlement, based on the full equality of all its inhabitants. Its governing body consisted of a council of twenty-four, elected by the six departments into which the community was sub-divided. These were: general economy, commerce, domestic economy, education, agriculture and manufacture. For a time this system worked well, but before long, disagreements began, and the constitution had to be re-organised; by 1830 the village had been split up into several independent units and the whole scheme eventually collapsed. Like many another idealist, Owen had not made sufficient allowance for the diversities of human nature. He was unable to make men remain equal, and his costly failure lost him more than four fifths of his private fortune, which he had used to finance the settlement.

In the 1840s, another experimental Village of Co-operation was tried, at Queenwood, in Hampshire. This was to be based on agriculture, and Owen aimed to make it a model village, well-planned and laid out, with well-designed buildings, the most modern equipment obtainable, and a fine new school open not only to the children of Queenwood's residents but to the children of Owenites from all parts of the country. But again the ideal came to nothing, ruined by squabbles and lack of funds, and by 1845 only the school was functioning. It continued to be run on Owenite lines for a further ten years.

Owen tried other ideas which he believed would bring about a change in the social system of his day. Still working on the principle that human labour-power could be calculated and rewarded, he suggested that workers should be paid in 'Labour Notes' instead of money. These Labour Notes could be used for the purchase of other commodities, the value of which was estimated by the amount of labour involved in their production, added to the cost of the materials required. Naturally enough, shops and markets would not accept the Labour Notes, and Owen hit upon the idea of buildings to which producers could bring their goods to sell and workers their Labour Notes to buy. The first of these was an 'Exchange Bazaar' in London. It was followed by a 'Labour Exchange' in Brighton and the 'National Equitable Labour Exchange', a purpose-built Exchange opened in 1832 in Gray's Inn Road, London.

It soon became obvious, however, that economic fluctuations made it impossible for the Owenites to fix an equitable price for many of their commodities. Some articles at the Labour Exchanges were priced too high, others too low; naturally, the ones which could be purchased more cheaply in ordinary markets did not sell, and the Labour Exchanges lost heavily. Once again, Owen's idealistic view of human nature played him false.

By the year 1833, a movement had started amongst various groups of workmen to combine together in groups or societies in order to protect themselves from exploitation by employers and generally to help one another. The employers, on their side, tried to prevent this by persuading Parliament to pass a series of laws—the Combination Acts—which made illegal such banding together of workmen in order to strike collective bargains with employers about their wages and conditions of employment. Trade Unions and Trade Clubs, however, continued to function and Owen, always ready to champion the workers, initiated the 'Consolidated Union' of all trades, which formulated its constitution and elected its first executive at a meeting held in London in February 1834. This, the forerunner of the modern Trades Union Congress, was an Owenite body, promulgating his views on the importance of Co-operation among workers, education for both children and adults, and mutual goodwill among members.

Owen, as usual, was prepared to move slowly, his first aim being to secure an eight-hour working day for all. The various branch unions, alarmed at the rapid increase in unemployment, were more anxious to force the employers' hands and strikes and demonstrations began, for which the Consolidated Union was blamed. In 1834, six Dorchester labourers, forming a lodge of the Friendly Society of Agricultural Workers, were convicted of administering an unlawful oath and sentenced to transportation. These unfortunate men were the 'Tolpuddle Martyrs', and Owen at once engaged in great activity on their behalf. In London, he headed a deputation of about 30,000 who marched to Whitehall to petition the Home Secretary to commute the sentence. Regiments of soldiers were called out to control the crowd but they were not needed. The demonstration was a perfectly peaceful one. The government, however, was alarmed at the potential power of the Consolidated Union and Lord Melbourne refused to receive the petition. The unhappy men of Tolpuddle were transported, many members of the Consolidated Union were cowed, and it began to disintegrate. Not for many years did the workers realise the strength that such a union could give them; after 1834 it was Chartism, rather than Co-operation, which became the guiding light of the labouring classes, and Owen's doctrines were almost forgotten.

In his old age, Robert Owen was very poor. He had spent his vast fortune on financing his various experiments in Socialism, both in England and in the United States, and eventually was living on an income of £360 a year, which his sons combined to allow him. He did not, however, cease his activities. A great deal of his time was spent in lecturing, both at home and abroad. He also wrote and published various papers and pamphlets setting out in detail his ideas on bringing about social reform—in 1848, that year of revolution, he was busily advising the French to adopt his Co-operative system—and he also wrote his own autobiography. At eighty-two he became a convert to Spiritualism, and from this time his mental powers showed a gradual decline.

He was quite certain that he conversed with all his old friends, and also with such personalities as Shakespeare, Napoleon and the prophet Daniel!

In 1853 his favourite son, Robert Dale Owen, decided that his father needed the peace and quiet of country life. He took rooms for him at Sevenoaks, and engaged an old friend of the early Owenite days, James Rigby, to care for him and take charge of his affairs.

In 1858, despite his obviously failing health, Owen travelled to Liverpool to address a meeting of the newly-formed National Association for the Promotion of Social Science. On the journey he was taken ill, but nevertheless he insisted on going to the meeting, where he had to be carried on to the platform by four policemen. He began his speech, but it soon became obvious that he was incapable of finishing it, and the chairman, Lord Brougham, applauded loudly in order to convince the old man that he had made his point, and then urged Rigby to get him to bed as soon as possible. He lay ill in Liverpool for a fortnight, then, miraculously as it seemed, recovered sufficiently to travel.

He obstinately refused, however, to return to Sevenoaks. His heart was set on revisiting Newtown, and there he went, to see the house where he was born. Rigby, seriously alarmed at his condition, sent for a doctor to attend to him at his hotel and hurried to fetch Robert Dale Owen, now the only person who had any control over his father.

While Rigby was away, Owen sent for the Rector of Newtown, with whom he arranged a series of meetings which he promised to address, and for whose benefit he set out a plan for re-organising the schools of the town. But when Rigby and Robert Dale Owen reached Newtown on the following day he was obviously very ill, and on 17 November 1858, he died. He was buried beside his parents in the old churchyard at Newtown, where his grave may still be seen. In 1902, the Co-operative Movement erected a railing around it and marked the spot with a memorial tablet to the man whom Lord Brougham once described as 'one of the most humane, simple-minded, amiable men on earth'.

Robert Owen's grave at Newtown

Lady Charlotte Guest, 1812–1895

Lady Charlotte Guest

Lady Charlotte Guest, who by her second marriage became Lady Charlotte Schreiber, was not Welsh by birth, but because of her work for the literature and culture of her adopted country, she deserves a place in the gallery of Welsh celebrities. She was the only daughter of General the Earl of Lindsay; her father, who was sixty-eight at the time of her birth, died before her seventh birthday. Her mother, many years younger than the General, soon re-married. She appears to have considered that a daughter required education only in the social niceties, as her ultimate destiny was to make a successful marriage, but Charlotte soon displayed an eager appetite for learning. She was an exceptionally clever girl, and by the time she was sixteen had taught herself French, Italian and German. She then persuaded her step-father to allow her to take lessons with her brothers' tutor, and added Greek, Latin, Hebrew and Persian to her repertoire of languages. She began to keep a diary at the age of ten, but, unlike the majority of enthusiastic children, continued her entries through her lifetime.

'From a child, I have always been anxious to retain the recollection of events,' she wrote when she was sixteen, 'but in my short experience, there is little to remember and little to forget.'

At least she was not over-conscious of her own cleverness. Probably her mother drummed into her that intelligence was no social asset—she must have found this bluestocking daughter an aggravating child. Charlotte was pretty enough; a portrait of her, painted when she was twenty, shows a pale, oval face, with a high forehead and delicate features, framed by smooth braids of dark hair. But would any man be prepared to take an interest in a young woman with so many formidable talents and so dogmatic a manner?

It was natural enough that Charlotte should not attract young men of her own age—she did not try. However, she met and married an older man who fully appreciated her exceptional intellectual powers. He was Mr. John Guest, a wealthy ironmaster, who was the owner of the vast Dowlais ironworks at Merthyr Tydfil. A Welshman by birth, he was almost forty-eight when he married Charlotte a few months after her twenty-first birthday. The age difference, however, did not matter to either of them. Guest, a civil engineer and a Fellow of the Royal Society, was not the type of man to choose an unintelligent wife. He accepted Charlotte as an active partner, and taught her a great deal about the manufacture of iron and steel, as well as the management of the Works, often acting on her advice in business matters.

She herself undertook to keep the accounts of the vast Dowlais concern, which at that time was producing 100,000 tons of iron annually. She taught herself the skill of double-entry, and her account books, with items written in a beautifully clear, flowing hand, always balanced exactly. Both husband and wife shared a deep sense of responsibility towards the Dowlais workpeople, building schools for their children as well as various places of worship, and ensuring that any sick or injured employees were well looked after. In return, they expected—and received—absolute loyalty.

Here, then, was Charlotte, a young matron in the early years of Victoria's reign, leading a life in many ways comparable to that of a well-educated young woman of today. In addition to her share in the management of the Dowlais Works, she was interested in Welsh culture, and when her husband became Merthyr Tydfil's first Member of Parliament, she accompanied him to London during Parliamentary sessions, meeting, as her journal shows, some of the leading figures of her time. Her account of a visit to the opera in the year of her marriage is particularly interesting.

Benjamin Disraeli, Earl of Beaconsfield

The young Disraeli was in the box; he and I soon got acquainted. We talked about several things. He is wild, enthusiastic and very poetical. The brilliancy of my companion infected me, and we ran on about poetry and Venice and Baghdad and Damascus, and my eyes lit up and my cheeks burned, and in the pauses of the beautiful music my words flowed almost as rapidly as his. Disraeli protested that repose was more important than anything else, and that nothing repaid exertion . . . yet noise and light are his fondest dreams, and nothing could compensate him for an obscure youth, not even a glorious old age. . . . I cannot understand him trying to get into Parliament.

Evidently she considered Disraeli's future to lie in the field of literature. They discussed contemporary writers—both were great admirers of the poetry of Southey—and he outlined to her the plot of his projected novel.

Disraeli appears to have appreciated the conversation of this intellectual young woman. They were together again when Lady Sykes took a party of friends to an Art Exhibition at Somerset House, and the clever young Jew sought her out, in order to air his views on art to a congenial listener. They remained friends for many years, for Disraeli eventually married the widow of Wyndham Lewis, a business associate of Charlotte's husband.

Always a linguist, Charlotte added Welsh to her repertoire. She read the *Mabinogion* in its original form, and decided to translate it into English, so that the Celtic version of the stories of King Arthur could be compared with Mallory's romances. This task took her eight years to complete, and caused her a great deal of heartache and humiliation. In the first place many people refused to believe that anyone, least of all a woman who had taught herself the language, could have mastered a text in obscure mediaeval Welsh. In the second, she suffered from the attempts of another scholar to plagiarise her work. But years later, Tennyson told one of her daughters that Lady Charlotte's *Mabinogion* formed the inspiration for his *Idylls of the King*.

On 30 November 1837, she wrote in her journal:

'Mr. Justice Bosanquet has, through Tegyd (her friend the bard, John Jones), kindly lent me his copy of the Llyfrcochyrhergest—the *Mabinogion*—which I hope to publish with an English translation, notes and pictorial illustrations. Pryce of Crickhowell and Tegyd have promised their assistance, and by God's blessing I hope I shall accomplish the undertaking. . . . The Welsh MSS Society wish to take the *Mabinogion* into their own hands. We have to arrange to prevent this, also to go into some plan for translating Justice Bosanquet's copy, as I do not feel inclined to give up my scheme of publishing it myself.'

Having made up her mind, Charlotte was not prepared to change it, but she was fair-minded, and made frequent acknowledgement in the texts to the help she received from other Welsh scholars, in particular the Rev. Thomas Pryce. She published her translation in three volumes, but often a long story—that of Geraint is an example— appeared at first in isolation, and Pryce would check the finer etymological points before her work went to press.

She spent a great deal of time on her translation, striving always to perfect her Welsh and not to be too dependent on the help of others, for she was determined that the new text was to be entirely her own. Publication delays worried her—she was of the type to demand speedy results—and she was meticulous in checking and re-checking her vocabulary, so that it should convey exact shades of meaning. In the end, her 'impatient patience' was rewarded, and her *Mabinogion* inspired a new interest in the study of Celtic Literature, not only in Britain but also in the United States.

The passionate interest shown by Lady Charlotte in her work is demonstrated by the two following extracts from her journal:

March 28th. Today I worked hard at the translation of Peredur. I had the pleasure of giving birth to my fifth child and third boy today.
March 30th. I was well enough in the afternoon to correct . . . one of the proof-sheets of my book, sent up by Rhys.

The stories of Arthur also formed part of the traditional literature of Brittany, and, as so frequently happens, a new cultural movement sprang up from more than one source, simultaneously. In the winter of 1838, Lady Charlotte was introduced to a young Breton writer, M. de Villemarque, who was attending the Abergavenny Cymreiggddion. He had been commissioned by the École de Chartres to study Welsh literature. At first, she was favourably impressed; he asked her to consider his translation of one of the lesser-known stories from the Breton version of the Arthurian cycle, and she included it, with proper acknowledgment, as one of the appendices to her first volume of the *Mabinogion*. She was annoyed, however, when de Villemarque persuaded her friend, Tegyd, to let him make a copy of the first draft of her translation of the legend of Peredur, for she discovered that he intended to publish it in France as soon as he could.

The matter may appear trivial on the surface, but it must be remembered that, while Lady Charlotte was translating from mediaeval Welsh into modern English, de Villemarque was merely translating her contemporary English into his contemporary French, a relatively simple task. Hers was the scholarly approach, and she was determined not to allow him to take the credit for research which he had not done. His aim was to get his French version of the legends published quickly; she, with that insistence on accuracy which she had already displayed in her book-keeping for her husband's Dowlais Works, would not submit any story for publication until she had verified her work from every source open to her.

Peredur, however, appeared in England before de Villemarque managed to rush his translation through the French press, and the fact gave her great satisfaction. This was increased when the Frenchman submitted an essay on the influence of Welsh traditions on the literature of Europe for a Welsh literary award, and did not even gain a mention for it. He had, however, drawn considerable material from her *Mabinogion* without acknowledging his sources. Later,

'he delicately insinuated that I did not write the book myself—a degree of moral turpitude which he dare not openly accuse me of. The secret of all this is his anger at not being able to forestall me in the publication of *Peredur*.'

De Villemarque, however, continued to make use of Lady Charlotte's *Mabinogion*, which he published in French under the title of *Contes Bretons*. She wrote angrily that he 'tried to make it appear that he translated it himself from the Welsh, without any obligation to my version.'

The literary wrangle continued for some time after the completion of *Mabinogion*, for many scholars were prepared to give considerable credit to De Villemarque's work, and Lady Charlotte had good reason to feel that she had been badly treated. *Contes Bretons* was well reviewed; she and her publisher did their best to expose the writer's dishonesty, and an explanatory article appeared in the *Quarterly Review*. The affair was of importance to only the two principals and a small number of Celtic scholars, and Lady Charlotte, satisfied that she had succeeded in making a significant contribution to the Welsh heritage, suddenly grew tired of fighting. A few months after the appearance of her third volume, she wrote:

Now that my seven babies are growing up and require so much attention, it is quite right that I should have done with authorship. I am quite content . . . and I am sure that, if a woman is to do her duty as a wife and mother, the less she meddles with pen and ink, the better.

This seems a very strange volte-face in the light of her previous enthusiasm and subsequent indignation. One may suppose that this unusual woman possessed a happy knack of seeing things in their correct perspective. Her aim had been to publish the *Mabinogion* in modern English, and this she had accomplished. She was sufficiently intelligent and open-minded to dismiss De Villemarque's intromission, and pass on to the next stage of her career.

Sir John Guest was by this time an ageing man. He felt that the responsibility of running the Dowlais Works was too great, but his relationship with his workpeople—he now had 12,000 families dependent upon him for employment—was one of benevolent paternalism, and he was reluctant to hand over to a manager. For several years Charlotte was an active partner in all his business undertakings, and when she eventually persuaded him to retire to Camford Manor in Dorsetshire, she made frequent visits to Wales to superintend the activities at Dowlais on her husband's behalf. He could not settle at Camford, however, and insisted on returning to his own land, where he died. His widow then took control of the Works into her own hands, and managed Dowlais successfully until the eldest of her five sons was capable of taking his father's place.

Three years later, Lady Charlotte Guest re-married. Her second husband, Mr. Charles Schreiber, was a fellow of Trinity College, Cambridge, and, like herself, came of a military family, for his father, Colonel James Schreiber, had served under the Duke of Wellington. This marriage, too, proved a singularly happy one. Charlotte was fortunate in that both her husbands appreciated her mental capacities and were happy to have a wife who was able to share their interests.

Charles Schreiber was a collector of porcelain, and Charlotte quickly learned a great deal about its manufacture and design. In 1865, she and her husband decided to make a collection of all types of English ceramic art. The objects were not to be chosen solely for their beauty, although there are some exquisite examples of colour and design among the pieces. Utilitarian articles, such as kitchenware in common use, also had their place, and the Schreibers scoured not only England but Europe as well in search of English pottery of all periods. Charlotte made a special study of the various makers' marks, which had not previously been classified, and in addtion to this, she did a great deal of research into early processes of making chinaware.

A tureen from Lady Charlotte's famous collection of English ceramic art, now in the Victoria and Albert Museum

In 1868, a factory was erected on the site of the old Bow porcelain works. When the foundations were being dug, many fragments of pottery were unearthed and also some of the original moulds. These were acquired by Lady Charlotte, and enabled her to identify many pieces of Bow china which had not previously been recognised as such, because they were of too early a date to carry a maker's mark. In 1870 she managed to purchase the memorandum books of one John Bowcock, who was employed at the Bow Works during the second half of the eighteenth century, and discovered in them references to some of those very moulds.

The proprietor of the Fulham works proved an enthusiastic helper. Inspired by

Lady Charlotte, he made a search of his records and discovered the notebook of Dwight, the original Fulham potter, in which were written down his methods for making 'white transparent porcelain, marbled porcelain etc.' at the time when he was working in London between 1689 and 1698. She was now able to identify Fulham pottery which dated back to the time of William and Mary.

Another entry in her journal records the acquisition in 1868 of a collection of examples of early Plymouth porcelain, which the descendants of the original potter gave to the Schreibers on condition that it should be kept in its entirety and never sold.

Her journals of this period are filled with enthusiastic notes about her hobby.

Paris, December, 1876. Madame Flandres has just returned from Italy, and has brought with her three Wedgwood heads, two of them Queen Charlotte and Catherine of Russia, most beautiful. They were irresistible. We had them for £16.

In 1884, Charles Schreiber died, and with the loss of her second husband, Lady Charlotte's enthusiasm for her hobby waned. She was, however, an expert on English porcelain and consequently well aware of the value of the collection. Realising what might happen to it should she herself die, she decided to offer it to the Victoria and Albert Museum, so that it should be preserved as a visual record of the history of British porcelain ware. This historical value would, of course, be lost if the pieces should be sold separately and dispersed.

In spite of her realisation that the Schreiber collection would form a permanent memorial to the work of her late husband and herself, Lady Charlotte's personal journal shows that she was sad when the beautiful pieces were finally removed for ever from her home.

November 19th. 1885. Before ten o'clock, the storekeepers from the South Kensington Museum arrived and worked all day. They had packed and carried all the Bow, and most of the Chelsea. I have been all day attending to the packers. Now my dear Chelsea aviary is gone. I close this sad volume with my adieu to my collection.

But Lady Charlotte was a born collector, and although she was now over seventy, her active mind soon fixed upon a new interest, this time, the collection of fans. She acquired fans from all countries and of all eras, and produced two lavishly-illustrated books on the history of fan-making, for private publication. Fans were, of course, still carried at evening functions by the ladies of the late nineteenth century, and were manufactured in Britain. She greatly admired the painted fans of pre-Revolutionary France, and tried to encourage similar work in this country by offering prizes in competitions for handmade, hand-painted fans. She was made an honorary member of the Fan-Makers' Company, and when her enthusiasm for this hobby waned, as it did within a few years, she gave

A plaque of Benjamin Franklin by Wedgwood and Bentley

Left: a plaque of Augusta of Saxe-Gotha, Princess Dowager of Wales, by Wedgwood. Right: a plaque of Queen Charlotte, by Wedgwood and Bentley. Both these plaques, together with the one on p. 63, are from Lady Charlotte's collection and are now in the Victoria and Albert Museum

all her fans to the British Museum.

The Museum also benefited from her last interest which absorbed her up to the time of her death. This was the history and design of playing cards. She sought out and purchased packs of as many different countries and periods as possible, noting and finding the reasons for the variations in their markings. The results of her research she published in three volumes. The first, *English, Scottish, Dutch and Flemish Cards*, and the second, *French and German Cards*, were published during her lifetime. The third book, *Swiss and Swedish Cards*, appeared in the year subsequent to her death, edited by a fellow-enthusiast, Sir Arthur Augustus Woolstone-Franks.

During the last year of her life, Lady Charlotte's sight began to fail, but she never lost her appetite for study. She was always in touch with contemporary antiquarians and collectors, and always ready to take an interest in their enthusiasms. She could not bear to be idle, and although no longer able to read or write, she could still manage to knit, and while she talked about antique prints or clocks with her friends, her fingers were busy making long red woollen mufflers for the London cabbies. She finished one a day and every month a parcel was despatched to one or other of the various cabmen's shelters.

Lady Charlotte died in 1895, her mind active to the last. During her eighty-three years she had seen many changes, but her passion for learning never left her. She left behind her two wonderful legacies of culture—the *Mabinogion*, in English so that the Arthurian legends could be easily read by anyone (and it is worth remembering that her work was the point from which modern research to discover the site of Camelot and the factual basis of the legends has grown) and the collection of china which demonstrates the unparalleled skill of the earliest English potters.

David Davies, 1818–1890

David Davies

Llandinam is a pleasant little village amongst the Montgomeryshire hills, on the main road between Llanidloes and Newtown. Born in this rural setting, on 18 December 1818, was David Davies, who was to become one of the wealthiest and most successful Welshmen who ever lived, landowner, mine-owner, engineer and philanthropist.

Though when he died he was one of the best-known men in the country, David Davies' beginnings were humble enough. His father rented a small hill farm named Draintewion, on the outskirts of the parish, and David was the eldest of nine children. Both his parents were industrious and hard-working, anxious to do their best for their family. They had a typical Welsh respect for the value of learning, and David was sent to the village school. This, of course, was before the days of state education, and Llandinam had no school building. The classes were held in the parish church, and had to be paid for. David was an intelligent boy who made rapid progress. By the time he was eleven years old he had absorbed all that the village school-master could teach him, but with eight younger brothers and sisters it was out of the question that he should be sent elsewhere. So, soon after his eleventh birthday, he began work as his father's assistant on the farm and, later, at the saw-pit, for his father worked as a sawyer to supplement his income.

The sawyers were important members of a rural community at that time, when many implements, as well as buildings, were still made of wood. Planks were sawn by hand, by two men using a double-handed pit saw, six feet in length. The tree-trunk to be sawn into planks was clamped lengthwise across a saw-pit, and both men worked on it, one, known as the 'bottom sawyer', standing in the pit, the other, the 'top sawyer', balancing on the log. The top-sawyer's work had to be very accurate. It was he who guided the long saw, kept the cuts straight and estimated the width of the planks. He was the man in charge of the operation, and young David Davies, who possessed a good eye and considerable physical strength, soon showed his talent for the work. He was known in the village as 'Davies Top-sawyer', and the nickname never left him.

Soon a second brother left school. The family finances improved and they moved to Neuaddfach, a larger farm in the same parish. But their good fortune was not destined to last. The father died, very suddenly, and David, not quite twenty, found himself faced with the responsibility of supporting his mother and the rest of his family.

Many a young man would have felt that this was too much for him to undertake, but David quietly stepped into his father's place as head of the household. With the help of his brother he ran the farm and also continued to work as a sawyer. He was shrewd, and had an eye for a good bargain. He made it his business to understand thoroughly everything to which he put his hand, and at that period in his life he understood timber. A local land-owner, Captain Crewe-Read, had on his estate a large oak tree which he wished to have cut down and disposed of. He told David Davies that, if he would do the job, he could have the tree for £5. David accepted the offer. The tree was felled and carted to the saw-pit, where he and another man sawed it into planks. When the timber was sold, he had realised a profit of £80.

David Davies quickly realised that, by utilising his knowledge, a man could become

prosperous. He understood timber and he understood farming, so in 1848, when he was thirty, he decided to strike out for himself. Leaving his mother and her youngest children at Neuaddfach, which he kept for her home as long as she lived, he took a much larger farm at Tynymaen. Everything he touched seemed to make money, and before long he could afford to run a third farm, Gwernerin, on the opposite bank of the Severn. Farming, however, was not his only interest, although he always supervised the organisation of his land. Like Thomas Telford, he was self-taught, and his interests, too, lay in what would now be termed civil engineering. At that time, a great number of smaller undertakings in road repair and construction were contracted out to local men. The County Surveyor gave instructions and made periodic checks, but in general left the work to the man on the spot, provided he was satisfied as to his reliability. David Davies already understood the use of wood and the construction of wooden buildings; he now began to study the use of stone, and before long was obtaining contracts for road repairs in and around Llandinam.

In 1850 he secured the contract to make a road bridge over the River Severn at Llandinam. His work satisfied the County Surveyor, a Mr. Penson, so well that he recommended the Montgomery County Council to pay Davies a sum of £15 over and above the amount agreed upon in the contract. He was probably also impressed by Davies' adherence to his religious principles, for the young man was a very strict Calvinistic Methodist, and all his life insisted on rigidly keeping holy the Sabbath Day. He would not even open letters on a Sunday, feeling that they were connected with work, which for that one day every week he must lay aside.

A story is told that, while he was working on the road and bridge at Llandinam, the

Surveyor drove on a Sunday from Welshpool, on purpose to see him about his work. The journey covered a distance of some twenty miles, taking a considerable amount of the official's time. He arrived while Davies was in Chapel, and sent in a message that he wished to consult him when the service was ended. The reply was that Mr. Davies would see the Surveyor on the following day, as he would not negotiate any work on a Sunday. He was young and ambitious; his refusal could have lost him further business, and he well knew it. But, although it meant a wasted journey, Mr. Penson was impressed.

All his life, David Davies was quick to grasp details. He had a facility for estimating costs rapidly, and was always quick to make up his mind. He was still a young man when Oswestry Borough decided upon the building of a new cattle-market, the Smithfield, and he was one of several contractors who applied. He went to Oswestry, where he was shown the plans and specifications, and was asked how long it would take to make up his mind before submitting an estimate of the cost for materials and labour. 'Five minutes', was his reply, and five minutes he took. The other contractors demanded several days. The job went to Davies.

In 1851 Davies married. His wife, Margaret Jones, came from Llanfair Caereinion, a small town not far from Llandinam, to the north of Welshpool. The marriage was a very happy one, lasting until his death, almost forty years later. They had one child, Edward, who inherited his father's vast business interests.

While working on the Oswestry Smith-field, Davis met Thomas Savin, who for a time became his partner. Savin was a railway engineer, and the mid-nineteenth century saw the high water mark of railway building, when rural areas were being linked to local market towns by this new and popular mode of transport, which enabled a journey to be made so much more quickly than by road. Each of the two men possessed great business acumen, coupled with inherent mechanical ability and a determination to succeed. They were jointly responsible for the construction of several railways in North Wales, the first of which was a twelve-mile stretch of line linking Llanidloes and Newtown. There was no railway within thirty miles of this area, the nearest station being at Oswestry. The materials needed for the work had to be brought to Newtown by canal, and when the line was completed the locomotives and carriages which were to run on it came up to Oswestry on their own steam and then had to be conveyed to Newtown by road, on huge specially-made wagons, each pulled by a team of ten horses. The line was opened for traffic in August 1859, but meanwhile Davies and Savin had built a shorter stretch, linking Rhyl and Denbigh.

By this time the partners were well known in Wales, and many other contracts came their way. Oswestry was linked to Newtown, and the line extended to Machynlleth and on to Aberystwyth. Savin then embarked upon an ambitious project. Not only did he plan to push the line on along the coast; he speculated on the prospect of a rush on the part of the general public to take seaside holidays, and began building large hotels at Aberystwyth, Borth and Aberdovey, which at that time were little more than fishing villages. But the great era of 'summer at the seaside' had not yet dawned. Savin's dream was in advance of his age; Davies was more practical. He tried to dissuade Savin from putting his development scheme into practice, and, when his friend would not give way, insisted on dissolving their partnership. Davies proved to be right, for in 1866 Savin became bankrupt. Davies, however, continued his work with other partners and became a director of the Cambrian Railways Company.

He was now a very rich man, and in 1864 bought for himself a large estate not far from Llandinam, commanding a beautiful view of the Severn Valley. Here he built a fine new house, Broneirion, which became the home of himself and his wife, and where, after his death, she spent the days of her widowhood.

By the time David Davies was forty-seven, he had already made a fortune, and although Broneirion was within sight of his birthplace, Draintewion, the difference in the style of living between the two homes was the difference of two worlds. Not that Davies ever allowed his wealth to alter his character. For the whole of his life, he retained the same standards of integrity, hard work and high principle; he was, however, now in a position to help those less fortunate than himself, and he was always liberal to anyone in whom he recognised a genuine will to succeed. He was a great believer in education, and remembering the brevity of his own schooldays, he paid for the building of a school and a school-house at Llandinam, so that the village children could receive free tuition. He also gave £6,000—a very large sum—towards the upkeep of the new University College of Aberystwyth.

In 1865 Davies turned his attention from the Cambrian Railways construction, although he remained a prominent member of the Board. Rich seams of coal had been discovered in Glamorgan, and, together with one or two of his friends, he purchased a piece of land at the head of the Rhondda Valley, where he sank a few experimental pit-shafts. The coal obtained was of very good quality, and ideal for industrial use, particularly for the smelting of iron. Davies decided to buy as much land as he could in the valley, for it seemed likely that the seam of coal extended for practically its entire length. The principal landowner in the Rhondda was at that time a Mr. Crawshay Bailey, who rented out a few hill-farms. As farm land, the valley was not productive, but Bailey had all the landowner's tradional suspicion of the rising industrial magnates, and stated roundly that he would not part with his land 'to speculators and adventurers'.

Davies' reply was typically forthright. 'Sir,' he said, 'I am no adventurer, but an honest trader, and for every honest guinea you will put down, I will put another.' Bailey was impressed; Davies bought the land and the fate of the Rhondda Valley was decided.

Much has been said and written about the despoliation of the Rhondda, and it must be accepted that different generations have differing viewpoints. Certainly Davies worked the coal seams in order to make himself rich. He also brought prosperity to a poor area, and, though despotic, was a benevolent employer. His miners were, for that period, well housed and fairly paid, and he cannot be blamed for the fact that subsequent owners did not keep pace with the advance of progress; houses and conditions considered good in his day were obviously below standard a century later. Moreover, he began his mines at a time when coal was in great demand; the tragedy of the Rhondda had its roots in the fact that that demand practically ceased. Davies was a man of high principle, who would have been horrified at the minimal wages and poor conditions prevailing in the valley fifty years after his death. In the golden hey-day of Victorian prosperity, he could have not foreseen the desolation which was to follow.

By 1873 there was a tremendous demand for Rhondda coal, both at home and abroad. There were seven pits, and their total output of coal every year averaged one and a half million tons. More than six thousand miners were kept in constant employment, and the annual wage-bill amounted to fifty thousand pounds. Davies and his partners formed themselves into a limited company, known as

Barry Dock and Island in 1895, six years after it was opened

The Ocean Coal Company. Of course, these vast stocks of coal had to be dispersed, and most of it went by rail to Cardiff docks, from which it was transported by sea.

It was at this juncture that the Ocean Coal Company came up against another monopoly. The only railway line running between the Rhondda and Cardiff belonged to the Taff Vale Railway Company while the sole owner of the dock accommodation for the export of coal was the Marquis of Bute. Both the Marquis and the Railway Company intended to take full advantage of the situation, and as the output of coal increased, so their charges soared. When the Ocean Company protested that excessive prices were being forced upon them, the Taff Vale Company reduced its number of coal trains and at the same time the dockyard facilities were restricted.

It seemed that an impasse had been reached, but Davies, though always prepared to strike a fair bargain and adhere to it, had an obstinate determination that no-one should take advantage of him. He had built roads and railways in the past; why should he not build a dock for his coal exports? A few miles to the South-West of Cardiff lay Barry Island. Once it had been a real island, the home of Giraldus Cambrensis' Norman ancestors; through the centuries, the channel between it and the mainland had silted up, and it was now a semi-derelict strip of shore jutting into the Bristol Channel, with a deep, curved bay which formed a natural harbour. David Davies planned to construct here a private dock, which was to be linked to the mines of the Rhondda by twenty-seven miles of a new railway, thus cutting out the use of the Taff Vale line and Cardiff docks.

Surveys were made, plans drawn up, and in November 1882 the Ocean Coal Company gave official notice of the project. But, even in the years prior to town planning, such an undertaking had to have Parliamentary backing, and a Bill to sanction the work was introduced early in the following year. It was hotly contested by Members with interests in the Taff Vale Rail Company, but after twenty-six days' acrimonious discussion it passed the House of Commons Committee, only to be rejected by the Lords' Committee, who were influenced by the Marquis of Bute. Davies was persistent. In the following year, the Bill was re-introduced. This time, the Lords' Committee spent thirty-three days discussing it, but at length it was passed, and in August, 1884, received the Royal assent. It had cost the Ocean Company £70,000 from first to last, but Davies was convinced that it was worth it, and events proved him correct.

It was he who was really responsible for getting the Bill through, for as chief shareholder he was constantly having to give evidence and to clarify various technical points. Money, of course, was a prime factor, and the capital of the Company was stated at one point to amount to £2,500,000. Davies was asked by a member of the Committee how, if necessary, this sum could be realised. The reply was characteristic. 'If the public will not come forward,' he declared, 'then I can find the whole of the money myself.'

The fact that no-one questioned the statement gives some measure of his wealth and of the confidence people had in his financial stability.

Work on the new dock was begun immediately, and in 1889 it was officially opened by Mr. Davies. Behind it grew up a complex of streets and houses and warehouses, for before long coal was not the only commodity to be exported. Modern Barry is a busy, industrial centre, with factories and shops as well as a large fairground which is one of the playgrounds of South Wales. But the bronze statue of David Davies still stands at the entrance to the original dockyard, a reminder of the fact that, but for him, this prosperous place might be still a sandy shore of dunes and marram grass.

Following the example of many other

The monument to David Davies in his native parish of Newtown

Victorian magnates, David Davies became a Member of Parliament. His first candidature was in 1865, when he stood as a Liberal for the county of Cardiganshire. His opponent, Sir Thomas Lloyd, was also a Liberal; the vote was split and Sir Thomas defeated him by a small majority. Some years later, Davies was returned unopposed as Member for the Cardigan Boroughs, which he continued to represent until, under the Reform Act of 1885, they were merged into the county. The Reform Act was followed by a General Election at which Davies once more stood for the county of Cardiganshire. On this occasion, his opponent was a Conservative over whom he gained a victory by over 2,000 votes. But he retained his seat for little over a year, for he opposed Gladstone's policy on Irish Home Rule, left the Liberal party, and joined the newly-formed Liberal Unionists, for whom he stood in the election which followed Gladstone's defeat. A Liberal stood against him, and won Cardiganshire by only nine votes. This was a particularly bitter contest in which party feeling ran high, and Davies, resentful of the fact that he had been beaten by such a narrow margin when he had been confident of victory, withdrew from politics altogether. Instead, he devoted his energies to local affairs, and was made a Justice of the Peace for Montgomeryshire in 1873 and County Councillor for Llandinam in 1889.

As he grew older, David Davies took more and more interest in local affairs, for despite his great financial empire, he always regarded Llandinam as his home. He gave very large sums to local charities, and although he never deviated from his own strict Calvinism he was not a bigot, remaining on good terms with the clergy of all denominations in his area. He was always ready to contribute towards either religious or educational causes, and frequently, if he heard of any small chapel in debt or needing money for repairs, or in order to maintain a Minister, he would pro-

vide it. He was once asked how much money he gave to religious charities in a year, and after a quick mental calculation answered that it was probably in the region of £10,000, but that he never troubled to keep an account of such gifts. If a genuine need arose, then he would provide the money.

He bought more land in and around Llandinam, and became one of the principal landowners of Montgomeryshire. He was a good landlord, always ready to improve property by erecting new outbuildings and paying for good drainage systems—both costly and necessary for farmland lying near to the Severn, always notorious for flooding. He never forgot his youth at Draintewion, and spoke to his tenants on a man-to-man basis, never attempting to intimidate anyone by his wealth and position in the county. As a result, his tenants always respected him and also showed him their gratitude for the fact that, although he paid for improvements to so many farms, he never increased the rents. Some of them, who remembered him as a young man, would proudly recount his feats of strength, for in his days at Tynymaen and Gwernerin it had been his habit, at times when the weather was too wet or snowy for outdoor work on the farms, to tour the sheds where the labourers had gathered for shelter. Many farmers, in these circumstances, used to send the men home, and that meant the loss of a day's pay. Instead, David Davies would organise what would now be called keep-fit classes, and joined with his labourers in weight-lifting, wrestling and other exercises.

On one thing he remained adamant all his life. He was a strict teetotaller, and would never allow either his servants or his guests any form of intoxicating drink. No home brewing was allowed on his farms, and, even at a harvest supper—one of the major celebrations of the countryman's year—though there was lavish provision of food, the only drinks supplied were water, milk or buttermilk.

All his life Davies was a man who enjoyed robust health, but when he was seventy he became ill and never fully recovered. In all probability, sixty years of unceasing work and responsibility had taken their toll, and for the last two years of his life he became a semi-invalid, confined to the warmth of Broneirion except on very sunny days, when he would be carried out into the garden. There he could sit and look over the valley towards his birthplace.

On 20 July 1890, he died, and was buried in Llandinam churchyard. He was so well known, and had so many interests in industry, farming and religion, that about 2,000 mourners filled the village on the day of his funeral. As a memorial to him a bronze statue, the replica of the one at Barry, was erected at Llandinam. But David Davies would have valued far more the comment of a local historian who, four years after his death, wrote of him: 'He ever manifested a broad, generous and unselfish spirit in all his dealings, and never did a mean or shabby thing to friend or foe.'

Ivor Novello, 1893–1951

Ivor Novello in 1933 in *Flies in the Sun*

Ivor Novello could, perhaps, be described as the last of the great actor managers, in the tradition of Irving, Tree and Forbes Robertson. For when, in his most triumphant years, he put on a show, he did everything—wrote, composed, directed, acted, selected his cast. Though he did not have his own company, in the sense that he always worked with the same players, whether in London or on tour, there was a nucleus of actors and actresses who appeared frequently in his productions, and who became his close friends.

He had many friends, and seems never to have quarrelled with anyone; he must have been completely free of malice or jealousy. Probably he never had occasion for either, for success came to him early in life, without the great struggle that so many young stage personalities have before they establish themselves. Success brought in its train wealth, in which he took an innocent pleasure, because it enabled him to do the things he enjoyed and to share his enjoyment with others. He is remembered not only as a brilliant, theatrical personality but as a gentle and generous person, of whom no-one writes or speaks unkindly. He had everything—good looks, charm, talent—and might well have become arrogant and domineering. He did neither, because, quite unconsciously, his life was dedicated to one thing only, his work.

One of the first, and certainly the most dominant, influences in Ivor's life was his mother, a professional singer of some repute, who was always billed as Madame Clara Novello Davies. Madame Clara was Welsh to her finger-tips, although she herself always hinted at some remote Spanish ancestry, dating back to the wreck of Armada ships off the Welsh coast. Her great-grand-father, the Rev. William Evans, was a Revivalist preacher famous for his eloquence, and she probably inherited some part of his forceful, flamboyant personality.

Clara herself was born in Cardiff, the adored only child of parents who, though by no means rich, were comfortably off. Both her father and her mother were musical, and she learned to play the piano and to sing as a matter of course. She was talented and something of an exhibitionist. Her father was the leader of a Welsh choir and she became his accompanist. When she was fourteen, she fell in love with one of the singers, a young man named David Davies, and demanded that they became engaged. Her mother, not unnaturally, refused, on the grounds that she was far too young. But Clara, characteristically, knew what she wanted, and eight years later she married him. By this time, she had formed her own Welsh Ladies' Choir and was making her reputation as a choral conductor; he had a pedestrian office job with the Cardiff City Council. David Davies never ceased to be astonished by his brilliant wife and, later, by his far more brilliant son. But he sought no share in their fame, content to remain an admiring spectator of both.

When Clara's first child, a daughter, died six weeks after birth, she was almost hysterical with grief and declared she would never have another baby. Before long, however, she realised that a second child was on its way. At first resentful, she later became reconciled to the event. This time, she hoped for a boy, and imagined him as being endowed with every gift, but especially that of music. The child was born on 15 January 1893, at the Davies' home in Cowbridge Rd. Cardiff. (Clara had romantically named the house 'Llwyn Yr Eos', which means 'Home of the Nightingales'.) It was a boy and as a baby his mother thought him far from handsome. His youth, however, fulfilled her dearest hopes; he had many gifts, and music was certainly the greatest of them. He was christened David Ivor Davies; one of the earliest marks of his great talent for giving pleasure to others was that he adopted his mother's stage name when he himself first began to play in public.

'Mam'—Madame Novello-Davies in about 1928

The early years of Ivor's childhood were punctuated by a series of abrupt partings from his mother, who was by now a celebrity, touring England and America with her Welsh Ladies' Choir. She must have been a dazzling figure to a child, in her gorgeous evening gowns, lavishly adorned with rings, bracelets, brooches, jewellery of any kind. Sometimes she would take him with her to a concert, where he would sit on someone's lap and watch her conduct her choir. When she opened a London studio in order to attract pupils from the capital, the child was often there. Many of his mother's clientele were

High Street, Cardiff, Ivor Novello's home town

members of the theatrical profession, and from them Ivor caught his passion for the stage.

At first, Madame Clara ignored this as a childish fancy, but when she discovered in the boy a streak of obstinacy matching her own she determined to wean him from the theatre before its hold became too strong. True, she wanted him to perform in public, but he was to be a singer, a pianist, a composer—in short, a musician, not an actor. He already had a clear soprano voice and, thanks to her, a facility for reading music. She entered him for a scholarship to Magdalen College Choir School.

His father objected, probably feeling that one musician in the family was more than enough. But Ivor was awarded the scholarship and went to Magdalen when he was ten years old.

Here he proved that he knew how to use his beautiful voice and developed an outstanding talent for music. He did not, however, lose his love of the stage. This was the era of 'picture-postcard' beauties and Ivor collected them all; Lily Elsie and Gertie Millar were his favourites. He also smuggled into school the scores of current operettas, which he longed to see. It is likely that Madame Clara knew nothing of this at the time, but she was delighted to discover that he was already beginning to compose music. This consoled her when his voice broke, quite suddenly, as sometimes happens. He remained at Magdalen until he was sixteen, when it was obvious that he would never develop a good tenor or baritone voice. He left school to become his mother's accompanist, and never sang in public again. His own parts in the famous musicals of his later years were invariably speaking ones.

His first song was published in 1910, and in 1911 it was included as a solo item in one of Madame Clara's concerts at the Albert Hall. Much against her wishes, Ivor insisted on accompanying the soloist himself: she objected, on the grounds that he was too inexperienced a performer for so large an auditorium. But her son could, on occasion, be stubborn. The song had a moderate success, but 'Mam's' judgment was correct. At that time both his talent as a composer and his touch at the keyboard were very light. He wrote several songs before his twenty-first birthday, of which one, 'The Little Damozel', is still performed.

The outbreak of the First World War, in 1914, made Ivor famous. Patriotic sentiments ran high, and Madame Clara urged him to write a patriotic song. The result was 'Keep The Home Fires Burning'. Ivor wrote the tune and some of the words, which were completed by his mother's American friend, Lena Guilbert Ford. It was first sung at a concert at the Alhambra Theatre; the composer accompanied the singer, the audience joined in the second chorus quite spontaneously, and it became the most famous of war songs.

Ivor's own war service could have proved a disaster, though it had its ludicrous side. He joined the Royal Naval Air Service in 1916, but during training was involved in two crashes in rapid succession. On each occasion, though he was lucky enough to be only slightly injured, the light plane was wrecked. The authorities decided that he was quite incapable of mastering the mechanics of flying, so he was transferred to a clerical post at the Air Ministry. Because of the success of 'Keep The Home Fires Burning' he found no difficulty in gaining access to the theatrical world, and wrote songs for several of the wartime revues and variety shows. By the end of the war, he had become an accepted composer of light music, but Ivor wanted more than this. He wanted to be on the stage itself; he wanted to act.

Certainly he had the looks for it, although it was 1921 before he appeared in a straight play. By this time he had acquired a flat in London, at No. 11 Aldwych, which was to be part of his background for the next thirty years. He had composed the scores for three musical comedies. His mother had become resigned to his place in the world of light music, though she always hoped for better things. And, during the early 1920s, parts on both stage and screen came to him, almost simultaneously and almost by chance.

The film was a comparatively new medium at the time, and casting was done in a very haphazard way. In 1919 a French director named Louis Mercanton, who was making a film, *The Call of the Blood*, was in London looking for an actor to play the role of the hero. Looking through photographs in an agent's office, he came across one of Ivor and immediately demanded that he should play the part. It was useless for the agent to explain that Ivor was not an actor, but a composer. Mercanton sent a cable to him in New York, where he was travelling with his mother. Ivor accepted the offer, and began his dramatic career in a film.

From then on he was dogged by a somewhat Ruritanian background which he accepted with cheerful enjoyment, although, when he himself wrote straight plays (as opposed to musicals) he avoided it. *The Call of the Blood* was a passionate melodrama of love and revenge, set in Sicily. It was filmed on location and achieved considerable success. On his return to London Ivor was offered a part in *Deburau*, a translation from the French writer, Sacha Guitry. From then on, for the next ten years, his work alternated between stage and screen.

He made two films for Mercanton, then English directors began to seek him out. There was a lavish production of *The Bohemian Girl* in 1921, in which he co-starred with the beautiful Gladys Cooper. Of course, gossip writers linked their names, for the menace of 'publicity value' was beginning to rear its ugly head, but both were too intent upon their respective careers to entertain any thoughts of romance. For serious actors, the stage was of first importance, the screen only a sideline.

In 1923, D. W. Griffith invited him to Hollywood to play the lead in a film called *The White Rose*. His good looks impressed the Americans, and some considered that he could rival the famous Rudolph Valentino. But, although he was always popular in America and enjoyed his visits to the States, Ivor never had the success there that he had in England. Perhaps he was too nice a person to stand up to the harsh ruthlessness of Hollywood's star system.

One of the people whom he met at this time was a leading actress of classical roles, Constance Collier. To her he confided that he was toying with the idea of writing a play; he had the ideas, but recognised the deficiency of his own knowledge of stage technique. They collaborated, under the nom de plume 'David L'Estrange'. The result, which appeared in London in 1924, was *The Rat*. Its success was phenomenal.

The story was set in the underworld of Paris where The Rat, an apache, lived on his wits. He was a ne'er-do-well, a loafer, who deceived both his wealthy mistress and the faithful little waif who loved him. He was the first of the anti-heroes, and Ivor Novello played the part magnificently, as he did again when, in the following year, it was made into a film. In 1928 he played the part once more in a follow-up film, *The Return of The Rat*, but by this time the novelty had worn off and the public wanted romantic heroes once again.

In 1926, 'David L'Estrange' wrote another play, *Downhill*, in which the hero deteriorates from a public schoolboy to a Marseilles dock-hand—of course, from the noblest motives. The same year, Ivor played the lead in a film-version of *The Lodger*, a novel by Mrs. Belloc Lowndes, based on the life of Jack The Ripper. He seemed in danger of becoming permanently type-cast.

In 1928, he wrote, produced and acted in his own play, *The Truth Game*, a light comedy. He still felt too uncertain to write under his own name, and the author was billed as 'H. E. S. Davidson'. He was encouraged by its success and, in 1929, there appeared the first play 'by Ivor Novello'. Its title was *Symphony In Two Flats*, and in it he really dealt with two plays in one. In one of the two flats lives a struggling young composer, tragically going blind, and his wife, who supports him while he is writing a symphony. Of course, there are misunderstandings, but the couple are reunited. As comic relief, the other flat is occupied by a widow and her two daughters, and their story turns on her attempts to find both girls rich husbands.

The amount of sheer, non-stop, hard work Ivor Novello packed into these years is incredible. He wrote *Symphony In Two Flats* while he was playing the part of Lewis Dodd in the first film version of *The Constant Nymph*. This book, a best-seller of the period, had already been made into a play, and Ivor was disappointed when he had not been asked to play Lewis Dodd. When the film-producer, Michael Balcon, first approached him he was inclined to refuse. But he had just seen a country house which he longed to buy as a retreat from London. It was Redroofs, near Maidenhead, and it was very expensive. So he struck a bargain with Michael Balcon; he would play the part if he were paid a sufficient sum to buy the house. And, as usual, he was lucky, for he got not only the house he wanted but the part he wanted, too.

Redroofs became a background for Ivor and for his many friends. They were real friends, too, for he had, amongst his varied talents, a talent for friendship. Lloyd Williams, his Welsh secretary, and Morgan, his Welsh chauffeur, never left him. Robert

Andrews, Lilian Braithwaite, Zena Dare and Olive Gilbert, amongst others, remained his friends for life. When one considers all the stories of backstage intrigue and spite, the happy atmosphere of Redroofs says much for Ivor's personality. His vices were two—cigarettes and coffee; drinking he considered unprofessional in an actor, and drug-taking was almost unheard of in the innocent years before the War. He collected at Redroofs various objects which had belonged to great actors of the past. The wrought iron gates from David Garrick's house screened one of the large windows. He also possessed some historic stage properties, one of which, a great star studded with brilliants which he wore pinned onto his dress uniform in *King's Rhapsody*, had once belonged to, successively, Edmund Keane and Sir Henry Irving.

There was, of course, constant speculation as to when, and whom, Ivor would marry. His name was linked with that of one famous actress after another, and his public could never understand why the gossip came to nothing. The reason, in retrospect, is simple enough; Ivor Novello was always in love. He was in love with success, with people, and, above all, with his work.

In 1931 his unassuming father died, but 'Mam' was frequently at Redroofs, advising, commanding, demanding. He never lost patience with her, though she became more domineering with advancing age. He never forgot that he owed to her his feeling for performance. It is interesting, however, to notice how many of his plays involve an ageing woman, sometimes very amusing, never pathetic, never ridiculous. Lady Mary in *Fresh Fields*, Donna in *Comedienne*, the Queen Mother in *King's Rhapsody*—all, perhaps, sprang from his infuriating, loving 'Mam'. She lived to share his triumphs and to see him doing what she had always wanted him to do, compose beautiful music which would be known to everyone. She died in 1943;

mercifully, she did not live to see him undergo the one really bitter experience of his life.

By the mid-1930s, when he was just over forty years of age, Ivor Novello seemed to have achieved everything an actor could wish. He had written plays and film-scripts and acted on both stage and screen. He was one of the idols of the theatre-going public. He had his London flat, his country home, his many friends. There was, however, one ambition still unrealised—to appear in a play of his own at the Theatre Royal, Drury Lane.

Drury Lane is probably the most famous theatre in the world, and at that period had the most complicated and modern effects. The lighting could be made to do almost anything, and so could the stage, which consisted not of one platform but several, which could be raised or lowered at differing speeds by complicated machinery in the basement. For years it had been occupied by American companies, who put on such spectacular shows as *Rose Marie*, *Showboat* and *Desert Song*. In 1930 Noel Coward managed to persuade the management to put on his poignant *Cavalcade*, which had a long and successful run. But after *Cavalcade*, nothing could take the public's fancy, and the manager, Harry Tennant, was in despair.

The story goes that Tennant was lunching with Ivor Novello and complaining bitterly about the series of losses at Drury Lane. Ivor, jokingly, suggested that he could write a show which would utilise all the theatre's resources. In the story there would be an opera, a revolution, a shipwreck and a gipsy wedding, all with a background of appropriate music and songs. Tennant told him that, if he could write such a show, it would be put on. The result was *Glamorous Night*, the first of the famous musicals with which Novello is always associated, even though his competent and frequently witty plays have been forgotten.

Ivor produced the script and the music. He was to appear in the play himself, though not in a singing part, and for his leading lady he chose Mary Ellis, who had already made her name as a singer on both sides of the Atlantic. He had composed some haunting tunes—the best known are probably 'Fold Your Wings' and 'Shine Through My Dreams'—and to write the lyrics he engaged a young man named Christopher Hassall, who was interested in theatre but who happened to be also a very good poet. His director was Leontine Sagan, a German who had already acquired an international reputation because of her handling of both stage and screen versions of the difficult *Mädchen In Uniform*. This team remained unchanged for four years.

Glamorous Night was a spectacular show. It included everything Ivor had promised, even the shipwreck, when, before the eyes of the audience, the liner Silver Star disintegrated and slowly sank, thanks to the skilful manipulation of Drury Lane's mechanical platforms, combined with clever use of lighting and sound effects. People were electrified, and it even gained royal acclaim, for King George V and Queen Mary went to see it and congratulated Ivor, though the King is said to have disliked the sad ending, on the grounds that he went to the theatre to be entertained.

Despite its success, *Glamorous Night* was taken off at Christmas, because Drury Lane always staged a pantomime. Ivor was, however, asked to write another musical to succeed it, and in 1936 came *Careless Rapture*. *Crest of the Wave* followed in 1937. This was the year of George VI's coronation; London was en fête, and Ivor matched the city's mood by including in the show a song, 'Rose of England', which before the end of the year was sung and whistled by almost everyone in the country. Determined to exploit Drury Lane's resources to the full, in one scene of

the play Ivor staged a realistic train crash.

The following year, Ivor briefly deserted the world of the musical for serious drama, taking the title role in Lewis Casson's production of *Henry V*. It was well staged and magnificently costumed, but so firmly was he fixed in the public's mind as the hero of musical extravaganza that he was never really accepted in a classical part. He enjoyed the short run, but was not unduly disappointed by the play's luke-warm reception, for he was working on another idea for Drury Lane.

The Drury Lane Theatre in 1937

This was *The Dancing Years*, which tells the life-story of Rudi Kleber, a Jewish musician who has fallen foul of the Nazis. In the opening scene, he is an old man, under sentence of death for helping others of his race to escape, and the audience sees his life in a series of flash-backs as he remembers his friends and his loves. Like many others, Ivor was aware of the plight of fellow-artistes in Hitler's Germany and Austria; perhaps his friendship with Leontine Sagan had helped to heighten his perception. The management of Drury Lane felt apprehensive about the political undertones of the theme, but the show went on shortly before the outbreak of War and the public loved it.

After the outbreak of the Second World War, Drury Lane was commandeered by E.N.S.A. and the play went on tour, to return to the Adelphi in 1942, where it ran for a further two years. It was during this period that Ivor came up against the experience which might have ruined his career and certainly made its mark on him for the rest of his life. The war was at its worst; almost all commodities were rationed, including petrol. Most people accepted the situation stoically, though a good deal of cheating did go on, and if offenders were caught, heavy fines were imposed. In 1944, Ivor Novello appeared before a London court, accused of obtaining petrol illegally. He always maintained that he did not know that it had been an illegal transaction; others were certainly involved. There was an appeal; the case dragged on. In the end, despite the fact that such outstanding personalities as Dame Sybil Thorndike testified on his behalf, he was sentenced to a month's imprisonment.

Most people felt that the sentence was harsh and unfair, for if he had not been a public figure he would probably have received no more than a heavy fine. Because he was so famous, the law made an example of him. He served his sentence, afterwards returning to play the part of Rudi in *The Dancing Years*, when the audience gave him a tremendous welcome. Some friends felt that, after a while, he put the whole affair behind him. Others thought that it embittered him,

others that it affected his health. Probably he brooded; he never made any public statement about the matter.

There were other musicals. Near the end of the war, in *Perchance To Dream*, he introduced 'We'll Gather Lilacs', a song which was to become as expressive of the emotions of the period as 'Keep The Home Fires Burning' had been, thirty years previously.

The last show in which Ivor himself appeared was *King's Rhapsody*, which he put on at the Palace Theatre in 1949. He had intended to write a musical about the Welsh National Eisteddfod, in memory of his mother, and had already composed part of the score, but put it aside when the new idea came to him.

The theme was as Ruritanian as ever—a misguided king, his mother, his mistress, and a beautiful princess whom he marries for diplomatic reasons. The songs were soon to become famous—one was 'Someday My Heart Will Awake'—and in the last scene Ivor, as the deposed king, stood alone in a huge cathedral after watching, incognito, the coronation of his son. Somehow, one remembered that silent, solitary figure.

The play had a long run. Ivor was tired; he left the cast for a few weeks' rest, returning, apparently refreshed, at the end of 1950. In March, 1951, he went back to his flat after the performance, complained of a pain in the chest, and collapsed. He died, of a coronary thrombosis, before a doctor could be called.

His death shocked everyone, for there could have been few in the country who were not familiar with his presence on-stage, or his face in films, or, more than all, his songs. But, beautiful as these are, it should not be forgotten that he could also write plays and act. Ivor Novello was a true man of the theatre.

Aneurin Bevan, 1897–1960

Aneurin Bevan in 1945

North Wales is a land of mountains and swiftly-flowing rivers, of small towns and seaside resorts, a place which attracts holiday-makers and where the majority of the inhabitants earn their living on sheep farms in the uplands or arable farms in the valleys. But the valleys of the South form a great contrast, for here coal seams lie, and in Monmouthshire and Glamorganshire, iron ore was mined. By the middle of the nineteenth century South Wales became the greatest iron-producing region in the world, with Ebbw Vale, Dowlais and the Rhondda Valley giving employment to thousands. The ensuing prosperity, however, was confined to the mine-owners, and from the days of the Rebecca Riots in the mid-1830s the South Wales miners, whose work was the hardest and most dangerous that could be imagined, showed a fierce resentment of this, even though many owners, like the Guests of Dowlais and David Davies, administered mines and factories in a philanthropic way.

By the end of the First World War the economic prosperity of the South Wales coalfield was beginning to decline, and foreign competition increased, so the decline worsened. Between the wars the miners in their small, primitive cottages in the despoiled valleys lived in a constant fear of unemployment which forced them to accept low wages. The majority of them were embittered by their sense of being exploited by the coal-owners. They were intelligent men, and it was largely from this bitterness that their traditional love of learning developed. A good education could help a man to escape from the mines.

It was in this environment, in Tredegar, that Aneurin Bevan was born, and against this social background that he grew up. Tredegar was a typical small mining town; it had a few imposing buildings, encrusted with the grime of the coal, but the miners' homes in 1897 were badly designed, sunless, and without running water. Small wonder that he developed a passionate hatred of the coal-owners and an equally passionate desire to improve the lot of the poor. Oddly enough, in the face of the squalor which confronted him throughout adolescence, he had an intense pride in Wales and his Welsh nationality, although, like Dylan Thomas, he never spoke his native tongue.

Aneurin Bevan's father had not always worked in the mines. At one time he had been a shepherd in the Carmarthen hills, but after his marriage poverty forced him to become a miner, as his own father had been. He worked hard, leaving home at five-thirty in the morning and seldom returning until after dark. He was a Baptist, unambitious, contented to spend what spare time he had in improving the little house in Charles St., Tredegar, where his family lived. Like many Welshmen, he possessed a good singing voice, and every Sunday would gather his young family around him in the parlour to sing hymns. He was treasurer of his miners' lodge and a Socialist, but with little hope that his political party would ever manage to improve the lot of men like himself.

He died a comparatively young man, of pneumoconiosis, a disease of the lungs caused by the inhalation of coal dust. No compensation was paid to his family; pneumoconiosis was not at that time classed as an industrial disease. His son remembered this, and when he became a Member of Parliament devoted much time and energy to assuring the poor of adequate medical attention and compensation to cover incapacities caused by occupational diseases, as well as by accidents.

Although Aneurin's mother was born in Tredegar her family came from Hay, on the English border. She was a very able woman, a good mother, insisting on high standards of behaviour. Her house was always kept in apple-pie order, her family well-fed and neatly clothed. What she managed to achieve on her husband's wage was little short of miraculous, for she had thirteen children in all, of whom ten lived to grow up. Above all, she was a great believer in education, always emphasising its importance as a factor in 'getting on in the world'.

Aneurin was David and Margaret Bevan's sixth child, and, like most children who come in the middle of a family, showed a strong and assertive individuality from the first. With his brothers and sisters, he went to Sirhowy, the local elementary school. His elder sister, Myfanwy, won a scholarship to the grammar school, and as Aneurin was obviously a clever child, his parents hoped that he would follow her example. But he hated school. Once he had mastered the basic skills, he was bored by formal education and his teachers considered him lazy. He stammered, too, and was teased about this defect, which he outgrew as a young man when he developed into a brilliant orator whose fluent Celtic rhetoric was later to impress both Parliamentarians and Trades Unionists. He was an omnivorous reader, devouring any material that came his way, from library books to comics. He was imaginative and quick at reasoning, but it seemed obvious that further education was not for him. When he was twelve he had a part-time job, working in a local butcher's shop on Saturdays and Sunday mornings. In 1911, as soon as he was fourteen, he left school and went to work in the mines.

The colliery at Tredegar at which Aneurin Bevan began work was known as Ty-tryst; the English translation is 'House of

The clock in the square at Tredegar (Bevan's town of birth)

where he made contact with others whose ideas and aims matched his own. At nineteen he was made chairman of his local Miners' Federation, which he represented in 1917 at a Federation Conference held at Cardiff, determined to bring about an improvement in the conditions of miners. The Miners' Union sent him to the Central Labour College in London, where he became a committed Socialist, but he rejected Communism because he disliked its repressive tendencies. In the years immediately following the Russian Revolution, he foresaw where wholehearted adoption of Marxism could lead.

He did not return to Ty-tryst, for the employers blacklisted him because of his avowed Socialism. For a time he worked as a labourer, road-building, watching the rise of unemployment as more and more miners were laid off during the economic recession which followed the cessation of war. He was involved in the General Strike of 1926, when the T.U.C. supported the miners in their fight against a reduction of wages. When the T.U.C. withdrew their support, Bevan backed the miners' leader, A. J. Cook, in his refusal to accept a compromise settlement. The miners continued their strike for several months, until they were forced by sheer poverty at starvation level to accept the lower wage. Bevan, because of his Union activities, became a marked man and for many years no-one would employ such a trouble-maker.

In the general election of 1929, he was elected as Member of Parliament for Ebbw Vale with a big majority. Authority might hate Bevan, but the miners trusted him, and never ceased to do so. Ten years later, when the Labour Party expelled him, the miners of Ebbw Vale again returned him as their Member, knowing that he was one of themselves and worked unceasingly for their good.

During the years of unemployment, the

Sadness'. At first, however, he did not find it an especially sad place. He brought home ten shillings a week, the wage for a boy. He was physically fit, he enjoyed the company of men like his father. And, joyously free of the drudgery of school, he began to educate himself in earnest. He wrote out his thoughts, he borrowed books from the local Workmen's Institute Library, reading not only fiction but scientific and political volumes. He stayed up late at night, digesting new ideas. For a time he continued to attend Sunday School, less for its religious instruction than for the chance it offered him to argue, pitting his theories against accepted dogma.

Then he joined the newly-formed local branch of the Independent Labour Party,

1930s, Bevan made his mark in Parliament as champion of the inarticulate poor. He frequently crossed swords with his leader, Ramsay MacDonald, and with Lloyd George, his fellow-countryman, both of whom he felt were too ready to compromise with the establishment. Winston Churchill, at that time in the political wilderness, had a strange admiration for the sincerity of the young, inexperienced Member from South Wales. He was the only Member to congratulate Bevan on his maiden speech, and although the two were so often at odds in later years, they never ceased to respect one another. The same qualities were to be seen in both—sincerity, flamboyance and a brilliant command of English. Bevan was also at one time an admirer of Oswald Mosley, though he opposed him bitterly when the latter left the Labour Party and formed the British Union of Fascists.

During the period immediately preceding the outbreak of the Second World War, Aneurin Bevan devoted himself to the cause of the socially deprived, the underpaid and the unemployed. Almost half of the adults in his constituency were out of work, and he angrily attacked the policy of employers who took on boys of fourteen, only to dismiss them as soon as they became old enough to earn a man's wage. He demanded help for the depressed areas, higher unemployment benefits and the abolition of the hated 'Means Test', by which a man's dole was reduced if another member of his family were earning. He was exasperated with the failure of the National Government to relieve the tragic situation in Jarrow, Merseyside and his own South Wales. He felt that they were sowing the seeds of a class warfare which would bring about their own destruction, and he did not hesitate to tell them so.

On foreign affairs he said little. It was Mussolini's invasion of Abyssinia which made him aware that there were other difficulties, apart from mass unemployment, to be faced. It was obvious that the League of Nations was unable to stop Mussolini's tactics and Bevan, like Churchill, saw that Hitler, too, was a potential threat to peace. With hindsight, it seems incredible that so few statesmen recognised the imminence of war. The country had never recovered from the ravages of 1914–1918; the majority simply refused to credit that such a catastrophe could recur. Bevan was one of the few who demanded, both in the Commons and at the Labour Party Conference, that the country should re-arm, so as to be in a position either to defend herself or to back the League of Nations with force when the need arose.

In 1936, Bevan backed Stafford Cripps in his attempt to form a United Front of all working-class parties—Labour, Independent Labour and British Communists—in an effort to win a Socialist majority in the next general election. Such a government, they felt, would be prepared to ameliorate social conditions at home and block the upsurge of Fascism abroad. But the Socialist leaders jibbed at the prospect of an alliance with Communism. They still relied largely on middle-class votes, and the policy of Cripps and Bevan was regarded as revolutionary. The United Front leaders were suspected of plotting with the Communists, and in 1939 Bevan and Cripps were expelled from the Labour Party. Bevan, recognising that he had been championing a useless cause, made his peace with the Executive and, after giving assurances that he would accept Party discipline, was re-instated. Stafford Cripps held aloof until 1945.

During this period, immediately previous to the outbreak of war, Bevan married. His wife, Jennie Lee, came, like himself, of mining stock and represented Cannock, a mining constituency. Their aims were basically the same. The marriage was a happy one, though, in those days long before the birth of 'Women's Lib', Jennie Lee shocked the public by refusing to be known as Mrs. Bevan.

This was the time of the Spanish Civil War, and Aneurin Bevan was one of the few politicians who saw it as a rehearsal for future events in Europe. On the invitation of the Republican Government, he and a few other Labour M.P's visited Spain in January, 1938, and returned with angry accounts of Mussolini's Italian bombers destroying roads and towns for Franco, their ally. Bevan said he was ashamed that the workers of Britain would do nothing to assist the workers of Spain. Throughout the stormy months of 1938 he fulminated against the advance of Fascism and Nazism, in vain; appeasement was in the air, and Bevan, like Churchill, was castigated as a war-monger.

When the Second World War broke out in September, 1939, a Coalition Government was formed. Prominent members of all Parties served in the Cabinet, amalgamating their talents in an effort to win the war. In this Parliament, which lasted until the end of hostilities, Aneurin Bevan was a backbencher. There was no opposition Party but the Member for Ebbw Vale managed to give his opinions on many controversial subjects and was listened to with an increasing degree of respect. Many Members disliked his views. He was, at various times, suspected of Communism or Pacifism, quite unjustly. Some, with more justice, accused him of deliberately trying to attract the notice of the public. But he was, with the exception of Churchill, the most brilliant speaker in the House, and, if he felt it necessary, did not hesitate to attack the leaders of his own party or even the Prime Minister himself.

One occasion on which he defied the leaders of his own party was in 1941, over the suppression of the Communist paper, the *Daily Worker*. The *Daily Worker* had published several leading articles urging British workers to sabotage the war effort, on the grounds that the war was essentially a struggle between imperialist powers, from which workers of all the countries involved should withdraw. When the British Communists urged a negotiated peace with Hitler, Herbert Morrison, the Home Secretary, himself a member of the Labour Party, suspended publication of the paper on the grounds that its views were an open incitement to treason. Bevan took up the cudgels on behalf of the *Daily Worker*, not because he was in agreement with its views—he was never a Communist—but because he regarded Morrison's action as a violation of the freedom of the press. This, he said, was one of the essentials of democracy, and if the Government prevented any minority from giving public expression to its beliefs, however unpopular, then Britain was no better than the Dictators against whom she was fighting. He moved a resolution against the suppression of the *Daily Worker*, but only six Members supported him, and this disinterested gesture made him very unpopular, for in the fervour of wartime emotions many people felt that he himself must have unpatriotic motives.

Throughout the war Bevan remained fundamentally loyal to Churchill, although he frequently criticised him on the floor of the House. Each recognised the genius of the other, and they resembled one another in that each had an almost fanatical belief in his own destiny. Because of this, Bevan continued to attack the Prime Minister on domestic issues, at the same time blaming his own party for not seizing the opportunities presented by war-time conditions for forcing the Government to carry out some of their ideals.

In 1941, the Member for Ebbw Vale was demanding the nationalisation of railways as part of the war effort. In a series of articles in the official Labour gazette, Tribune, he called upon the Government to take over all land which was not under cultivation, and in the House of Commons he suddenly demanded the closure of all Public Schools as a step towards the abolition of class privilege. This had the effect of infuriating many Socialists, as well as the Conservative party. He accused the Government of not sending enough help to Russia in her struggle to hold back the invading Nazis, and continually demanded a second front in Europe, long before the country was in a position to mount a full-scale invasion. His arguments during the war years were frequently mistaken and misguided, but his sincerity could not be doubted. He had never forgotten the conditions of the unemployed, poverty-stricken Welsh miners of pre-war years, and was determined that such conditions should never return.

In 1945, after the cessation of hostilities, a General Election was held, the first since the outbreak of war. The Coalition Government had lasted for seven years; now party politics were resumed, and a Socialist Government was returned with a very large majority. The new Prime Minister was Clement Attlee, an intelligent, unassuming man who knew how to delegate authority to the persons most suited for it. He recognised Bevan's real vocation—the cause of the underprivileged—and, despite the opposition of some of his Cabinet Colleagues, appointed him as Minister of Health and Housing.

Attlee knew very well that Aneurin Bevan was the one man of all others with sufficient dedication to carry through the Socialist ideal of free medicine for all. The plan was not completely new. During the early years of the war a Liberal, Sir William

Ebbw Vale, for which Bevan was elected Member of Parliament in 1929

Beveridge, had published a report on the possibilities of a National Insurance Scheme, by means of which all citizens, through contributions made during their working lives, would be enabled to provide against sickness, unemployment and old age. The 'Beveridge Plan', as it was called, made a tremendous impact on the public, and it formed the basis for Aneurin Bevan's National Health Service Act of 1948. He began working on it in 1946, but it was two years before he could get the Commons to ratify his Bill. The fiery Member for Ebbw Vale could be patient when necessary.

It is difficult for those who have lived with the National Health Service to realise what life was like without it. Aneurin Bevan knew it all; his father had died after a long illness, and an illness had to be paid for. Every family, apart from the wealthy, lived in the dread of two great fears, unemployment and illness. Unemployment pay was low, but doctors' fees were high. The very poor, 'on the panel', paid less, but the majority of people were terrified at the possibility of a long illness, with all the expense it entailed—loss of earnings, doctor's bills, hospital fees, extra foods. Bevan had seen it time and time again, in his own constituency as well as in his own family. Now he had the opportunity to rectify this state of affairs by providing free medical care for all.

He was convinced that the majority of the public, whatever their political opinions, would welcome the scheme. In a brilliantly-written pamphlet, 'In Place of Fear', he explained his plan. Medical treatment should no longer be in the hands of private practitioners, hospital treatment should no longer depend on a person's ability to pay for it. Instead, every citizen should make a fixed contribution, deducted regularly from his earnings. From the total of these contributions, doctors and hospitals should be financed by the state. In return, any citizen

Unemployed Welsh miners during the depression of the 1930's

who became ill would receive such treatment as was necessary, but the treatment should not be looked upon as 'free medical care', because it had already been paid for by the contributions.

At first, the British Medical Association was strongly opposed to the scheme, and Bevan's political opponents watched with interest, waiting for him to lose his temper and declare open war on the doctors. But Bevan did nothing of the kind; when he wanted a thing, he could afford to wait, and gradually he won the majority of the doctors over. The Health Act was passed.

But although he kept cool in his negotiations with the B.M.A., Bevan did lose his temper with his political opponents, and it was at this time that he made an angry and ill-judged speech in which he referred to the Conservatives as 'lower than vermin'. They never forgave him, and the expression dogged the remainder of his political career.

In housing, he displayed competence. There was a great shortage of houses after the war, partly as a result of the Nazi bombing attacks, partly because so many people were moving from one part of the country to another in search of new jobs. He encouraged local councils to build subsidised houses for rent, but he also encouraged people to buy their own homes. Some Socialists were against this, but he stated openly that, in his opinion, there was nothing ant-Socialist in home-ownership.

He disagreed violently with his party's foreign policy, which he felt was too much influenced by American capitalism. Together with other Left-wing Socialists, he openly deplored the acceptance of American financial aid towards Britain's recovery from the economic disasters following the war. In 1951 he resigned from the Labour Government, which had been re-elected, though with a greatly reduced majority. After the fall of the Government, Attlee resigned the leadership, and Bevan made a bid to be chosen in his place. He failed, however; the more moderate Hugh Gaitskell was elected, and, after his premature death, was succeeded by Harold Wilson.

By 1957, much of Aneurin Bevan's initial fire had gone out of him. His attitude to politics had matured, and as deputy leader of the Labour Party he served as a loyal and temperate member of the Opposition. He had longed for political power, but the supremacy of leadership had been denied him. He and his wife now divided their time between London and their country home in Buckinghamshire, where he took a pride in rearing prize pigs. But he paid frequent visits to Tredegar and Ebbw Vale, where the miners continued to give him their support, eagerly acknowledging all that he had done for them.

There was dissention in the Labour Party; he might have yet have become its leader. But in December, 1959, he was suddenly taken ill, and he never regained his former vigour. In July 1960 he died, at the early age of sixty-two, surely one of the most colourful figures ever to enhance the Parliamentary scene. It was impossible to be neutral about Aneurin Bevan; people either idolised him or loathed him. But it is certain that, with his passing, a certain element of greatness also passed from British politics.

Dylan Thomas, 1914–1953

Dylan Thomas

Dylan Thomas is probably the most familiar name amongst poets of the post-war years. Although few readers make a profound study of his work, most people are able to quote from *Under Milk Wood*, 'Do Not Go Gladly', and 'Death Shall Have no Dominion'. The bare facts of his life are still discussed— the drinking-bouts, the unconventionality, the fecklessness, all of which contribute to the picture of the typical Bohemian. Yet few knew him intimately, while those who fully understand the background to his work are even fewer. Only Browning matched him in his tempestuous love of words, only Donne in his understanding of the day-to-day suffering of humanity. And both these qualities, in which the greatness of his work is rooted, stem from his Celtic background.

His father, D. J. Thomas, was the English master at Swansea Grammar school. A scholarly man, he himself had longed for recognition as a bard. But he was a strange contradiction in character; born of Welsh-speaking parents and brought up in a Welsh-speaking home, he refused to use the language after he left his University, and did not teach his children their native tongue, so Dylan Thomas never spoke Welsh, although he understood it. His mother, Florence Williams, was a farmer's daughter from South Wales. She, too, dropped the use of Welsh after her marriage; Dylan's education was basically English although behind him lay a mass of Celtic tradition and culture.

He was born in his parents' home, No. 5, Cwymdonkin Drive, Swansea, on 27 October 1914. He was the second of their two children, his sister, Nancy, being his senior by nine years.

It is interesting to note that his father, having already rejected the Welsh language, returned to it when choosing a name for his son. An uncle, Gwylym Thomas, had once been awarded a bardic chair and, as was the custom, had been given a bardic name—Marlais, which was the name of a river. 'Dylan' is taken from the *Mabinogion*, that treasury of Welsh folk-lore, one of whose heroes is Dylan Eil Ton, meaning 'Son of the Sea-wave'. During 1914 an opera based on his story had been staged at Covent Garden, in an attempt to link Welsh literature with the Irish Celtic Revival, emanating from Dublin's Abbey Theatre. Dylan's father must have been aware of this, and his fundamental sense of his own nationality prompted him to give his only son the names of a Welsh bard and of a Welsh legendary hero. Neither name was in common use at the time.

The poet's childhood was a happy one, although his parents differed greatly in background and in personality. His father laid great emphasis upon an academic education, yet was very tolerant when his son refused to go to a university. A scholar himself, he filled the house with books, and the boy became an avid reader at a very early age. His mother, who came of country stock, had many relatives who were farmers. Dylan's summer holidays were usually spent at Fern Hill, Llangain, where his Aunt Ann and Uncle Jack lived. Here, he absorbed the spirit of the countryside as seen through the eyes of a not very efficient tenant farmer. He lazed, he wandered, he watched; he never forgot Fern Hill.

Sometimes, he was sent to stay with another aunt, whose husband, the Reverend Dai Rees, was the Minister of the Paraclete Chapel at Newton. There he would be sent to Sunday School, and from his Uncle Dai he acquired his vast background of biblical stories and language, for no-one knows his bible better than a Welsh minister, and the resounding phrases of the Hebrew psalms lost little by being translated into Welsh.

The Arts and Crafts Public Library in Swansea in 1928

The Williams' were a closely-knit family, and there were frequent visits to Swansea. Dylan, who had no cousins of his own age, seems to have been indulged by his mother and his aunts. He was a delicate child, very subject to colds, coughs and bronchitis. He also had brittle bones, which an ordinary tumble could easily snap. Even as a man, he frequently broke wrist or arm as the result of a fall. Until he was seven, he was not sent to school, but his father taught him at home. Both parents spoiled him, his mother especially waiting on him hand and foot, which must account for a large measure of his helpless and generally unpractical nature in adult life. Thanks to his father, he acquired a wide background of literature when he was very young, for his bedtime stories came from books prescribed for the Grammar School's examination syllabus.

The sea was a mile or more from Dylan's home, so as a child he was not often taken to the beach. There was, however, a park very near, and this was his favourite play-place. A carved stone, erected in 1963, now stands there as a memorial to him.

When he was seven, he was sent to a small private school near to his home, and remained there until he went to Swansea Grammar School at the age of ten. It is doubtful whether he learned much of value at his first school. He appears to have been a very normal small boy, given to fighting, cheating and illicit smoking of purloined cigarettes.

He did, however, discover two things about himself. One was that he enjoyed writing things down, anything that came into his head. The other was that he was a born actor. He never outgrew his delight in taking part in a play; had he not become a poet, he would probably have gone on the stage.

At the Grammar School, Dylan began to show those traits of character which were maintained during his adult life. He was small and not robust; his mother had always pampered him. One would have expected such a boy to become a target for bullying, but strangely enough he did not. He was always confident that somebody or other would look after him, take his part and get him out of scrapes, and, oddly enough, someone always did. He was given to extremes; if he were naturally good at a subject, he worked at it and did well, but if he could not excel, then he was quite happy to be at the bottom of the class. For him, there was no middle way, and he was too lazy to work hard in order to master subjects which he found difficult.

The result was that, English apart, his academic record was a very undistinguished one. He read a great deal of poetry, wrote some, and became the Editor of the School Magazine. He also took the lead in the school plays, for, in addition to his dramatic talent he possessed a beautiful speaking voice. When he was sixteen, he left school, determined to become a poet.

His parents' reaction to this somewhat unconventional ambition was an unusual one. Probably his father recognised, even then, that his son had the makings of literary greatness in him. His mother, who still worried over his delicate constitution, was glad that he should continue to live at home, where she could look after him. Neither parent seems to have mentioned the difficulty of making a living by writing poems, though Dylan did get himself a job, as a very junior reporter on the staff of the local paper.

He himself was at the time in the grip of a passionate admiration for Keats, on whom he modelled himself. He was always something of a hypochondriac; now, remembering his many childhood illnesses, he convinced himself that he, too, would die young. He was already a heavy smoker and had developed a rasping cough, which, all his life, he half-believed to be a symptom of tuberculosis. He may have had a tendency to this disease, far more common in the 1930s than now, but it was certainly not the cause of his death, and a born exhibitionist, he enjoyed his fantasies of himself as a doomed poet.

For the next three years he remained at home, worked as a journalist and wrote a great deal of poetry. He was, of course, lucky to have a job at all, for this was the period of the great Depression, and he cannot fail to have been affected by the sight of his contemporaries standing in the dole queues. For a time he made a real effort to learn how to succeed as a journalist but, as with school subjects which he did not find interesting, his attention frequently wandered and he spent much of his time day-dreaming. He insisted on writing to please himself, but what pleased Dylan did not always please his editor, who dispensed with his services after two years.

He did a great deal of acting at this time, taking part in plays put on at the Swansea Little Theatre. Older citizens of Swansea considered the repertoire of the Little Theatre to be too avant-garde, but for an amateur company they did very well, and several of them, including Dylan, seriously considered the stage as a career. He made many friends during this period of late adolescence, and they remained friends throughout his life. For he possessed an undeniable charm and sincerity under all his poses and his unreliability and his many weaknesses, and once people were attuned to these qualities they were prepared to overlook his many defects.

It cannot be denied that, before he was nineteen, he had developed into a heavy drinker, and remained so. A great deal has been said about his drinking, which many Welsh Nonconformists found particularly shocking. The habit undeniably damaged his health and affected his personal relationships; he seemed incapable of making any effort to control it. Yet he never drank while he was writing; he was well aware that to do so would impair his perceptive faculties. Even in manhood, he remained in many ways immature. He drank partly in order to gain a temporary escape from the harsh facts of life, and later, when he became famous, he drank because it was expected of him. Having created for himself the role of the drunken poet, he must live up to it.

In 1933, Dylan's sister married and went to live near London. That year, he visited her. It was the first time he had been to the capital, and he made the most of it; indeed, considering his basic inefficiency in practical matters, he made remarkably good use of his time. He had had only one poem published in a London periodical—'And Death Shall Have No Dominion' had appeared in the *New English Weekly.* He visited several editors and made contact with the publishers Faber and Faber, who were one of the few firms prepared to take a risk with unknown poets of promise. (Eventually, though, it was Dent who published most of his early work.)

After his return to Swansea, he began to send more and more of his poems, short stories and essays to literary magazines. Some were accepted, but many were not; his style was considered to be highly unconventional. Rejections depressed him. Indeed, during the first half of 1934, while he was making so much effort to establish himself as a poet of standing, he became almost neurotic. He did, however, win a major prize offered by a London paper, the *Sunday Referee,* which included the publication of a collection of his poems. He set about selecting and preparing these, and left Swansea to live in London in November, 1934.

He rented a room on the fringes of Soho, which at that time stood in relation to London much as the Latin Quarter did to Paris. It was international in character, and its many pubs and small, foreign restaurants were frequented by unknown young writers and artists, trying to establish themselves. Food was cheap, drink sometimes cheaper, and the Bohemian habitués were tolerant of all and any eccentricities. Major celebrities could be found there, too, dining and wining at the old Café Royal.

Dylan enjoyed himself during his Soho days. He felt that he was freeing himself from his conventional upbringing. But it is interesting to note that, at frequent intervals, he would return to the safety of his parents' house in Swansea. At heart he was always a moralist, a religious man who followed no acknowledged creed. His drinking, his heavy smoking, were a pose he adopted and most of his stories about the excesses of his London life remained nothing but stories. He acted out a part to himself and to his friends, and continued to do so for the rest of his life. But he was never prepared to be insincere about his work. He wrote as he felt, using the style which seemed to him right. In many ways, he was humble about his writing, prepared to listen to advice. But always he remained the ultimate arbiter of his own words, and in that field, no compromise was ever permitted.

He was a meticulous craftsman, too. The casual reader often misses a part of the depth of meaning in his work because his words flow so easily, like a stream tumbling over rocks. But that apparently effortless cascade of condensed images and double meanings was not achieved without intense concentration. Like his childhood model, Keats, Dylan Thomas would go over a poem again and again, crossing out, substituting, making marginal notes. He would discard one draft after another until he was satisfied, and when he was satisfied he was always mentally exhausted, and took refuge in drink, or exhibitionism, or a return to Swansea.

Eighteen Poems, published soon after he arrived in London, was almost unnoticed by reviewers. It appealed, however, to some discriminating readers, among them Margaret Taylor, the wife of A. J. P. Taylor, the historian. She became a lifelong friend, often helping Dylan in later years, when family and financial problems proved too much for his failing health. Another friend was the poet Vernon Watkins, one of the few men from whom Dylan was prepared to take advice. In 1936, after the publication of his second book of poems, he met Dame Edith Sitwell, who admired his work and did a great deal to further his career. It is interesting to note that perceptive writers of this calibre saw beyond Dylan's façade to the integrity of the poet; in his turn, he neither attempted to impose upon them, nor did he behave badly when he was in their company.

Dylan first met his wife, Caitlin Macnamara, in 1936. The daughter of an impoverished, though aristocratic, Irish father and a French mother, her background and upbringing had been vastly different from his own. Her parents parted shortly after her birth, and she and her sister grew up in the unconventional ambience of the artist, Augustus John, whose large family became their neighbours and close friends. She was a beautiful girl, with fair hair and wide blue eyes, clever, though more or less uneducated, for she spent very little time at school. She spoke French fluently, read widely but without discrimination, and became a freestyle dancer in the vogue set earlier by Isadora Duncan.

Dylan and Caitlin fell in love at their first meeting, and, despite the various traumas of their marriage, that love survived. She was always his refuge; the fear of losing her was the greatest of his many fears. She in her turn never ceased to love the poet in him, though towards the end of his life, when, as she saw it, he was prepared to compromise with commercialism, the weakness of the man infuriated her.

They were married the following summer, without giving any thought to the consequences. Neither had money and Dylan's earnings were small. He had been quite happy, in his bachelor days, to live in London without any base, if need be, eating in pubs and sleeping on the floors of his friends' studios. But now he had a wife he needed a home, and he could not afford one. They lived first with his parents, then with Caitlin's mother. In 1938, they rented a cottage in the little fishing village of Laugharne.

Laugharne, a tumble-down place with no industry, no attraction for tourists, falling between English and Welsh cultures, became Dylan's spiritual home. Like him, it had no established background; although he left it, he returned again and again. It became Llareggub in his best-known work, *Under Milk Wood*.

During the year preceding the outbreak of the Second World War, Dylan's output increased and he began to be known not only as a poet but also as a writer of short stories. He also did one or two broadcast talks for the

BBC which, thanks to his natural dramatic talent and his beautiful speaking voice, were successful. But after his first child was born, he could not afford even the cottage at Laugharne, and once more they went to live with Caitlin's mother.

Dylan's attitude towards the war was unequivocal. He said openly that he had no wish to fight. But his reasons were varied. He was a pacifist, but neither politics nor religion entered into his conviction. It has been suggested that he was a Communist, but this was not the case, apart from the fact that, in his Swansea days, he talked a great deal about Marx and idealistic Communism, as the young do. The Spanish Civil War affected him, but he never contemplated following the example of many of his contemporaries and going to fight in Spain. He never made any pretence that his religious views kept him out of the armed forces: certainly, he did not want to kill, but he said openly that his instinct for self-preservation drove him to make certain that he himself was not killed. Like many young men of his generation, brought up in the shadow of the 1914–1918 war, he felt, when war broke out in 1939, that he had been let down by the statesmen. The war was, in his view, an unsought interruption in his life, and he wanted no part in it. Yet, perversely, when he attended a tribunal for conscientious objectors, he despised those who pleaded for exemption on religious grounds. He could, however, have spared himself a great deal of soul-searching, for an army medical examination rated him C3—unfit for active service.

Eventually, Dylan found himself in a more or less reserved occupation. In 1940 he was writing scripts for the BBC's Latin American Service. He also wrote some film-scripts for the Ministry of Information, and so found his way into the world of films.

From 1940 to 1949, he did a great deal of film work, first for the Ministry of Information and then for Gainsborough Films. His scripts were original and conscientiously written. Unfortunately, owing to the unsettled conditions prevailing in the film industry during the war, many of them never reached the screen. His private life, too, was unsettled. In 1942 he rented a studio for Caitlin and himself in Chelsea; their second child, Aeronwy, was born. But the blitz made London unsafe for babies, and once more Caitlin and the children went to her mother's house in the South of England. Left alone in London, Dylan was very lonely. He sought company of any kind; he read only for relaxation, so that his literary background deteriorated steadily. Though he was now, for the first time in his life, earning a regular income, the money ran through his fingers like water. He was as poor as ever, and he wrote very little poetry.

At the end of the war, he had nowhere to live, and was desperately trying to find a place where he, Caitlin and the children could be together. Worn out with fruitless journeys between Swansea, Ringwood and London, coupled with the effort required to publish, early in 1946, a fourth volume of poems, he collapsed from nervous exhaustion and had to spend a month in a London Hospital. When he was discharged, Margaret Taylor came to his help. Her husband was now at Oxford, and she offered Dylan and Caitlin a wooden summer-house in their Holywell garden as a temporary home. They remained there for more than a year.

This was the period during which Dylan gained his reputation as a broadcaster. The BBC was launching the Third Programme, which was to be devoted to the Arts, and writers and musicians, both the famous and the little-known, contributed to it. Dylan's acting ability, coupled with his beautiful speaking voice, soon made him a popular radio presence. He also made some recordings

The Boat House in Laugharne, where the Thomas family
lived from 1949

of his own poems, which were being published
in the United States at that time, and in 1947
was awarded a Travelling Scholarship by the
Authors' Society. This took him to Italy,
which disappointed him, although while he
was there he managed to rest and to write
poetry, as opposed to scripts for radio and
films.

On his return to England, however, he
was once more in financial difficulties, this
time with the Inland Revenue. For some
years now he had been earning a reasonable
salary from both Gainsborough Films and the
BBC, although the royalties from his books
remained small. With his usual disregard for
money matters he had spent freely, without

declaring his income for tax purposes or
making any provision for payment in the
future. Now the inevitable demand came,
and for a very large sum, far more than he
could possibly pay. His friends managed to
induce the Inland Revenue to spread out the
payments over several years, but from 1949
up to the end of his life most of what he
earned was already earmarked to meet this
debt. One of the main reasons for his strenu-
ous American tours was to get money in
order to pay it.

In 1949, Margaret Taylor bought the
Boat House at Laugharne, and Dylan and
his family moved there on payment of a very
nominal rent. His parents also moved to
Laugharne. His father had retired—he was,
in fact, a very sick man—and Dylan felt that
he would like them near at hand. One of the
unexpected and endearing traits of his
character is this very real sense of family
obligation. In their turn his parents, though
they might disapprove of his way of life,
always retained their affection for him; his
father in particular appreciated the merit of
his poetry and was immensely proud of him.

It was at Laugharne that he wrote his
last poems and completed *Under Milk Wood*,
though it is doubtful whether Dylan himself
ever regarded it as complete. He revised it
many times and was never entirely satisfied
with it.

Laugharne proved restful to his mind,
but, although no-one was really aware of the
fact, physically he was a very sick man. It is
only during recent years that alcoholism has
been recognised as a disease; twenty-five
years ago, it was regarded as a perverse form
of self-indulgence which could be cured by
will-power. In addition to the physical consequences of drinking, his lungs were in a bad
state; this had been a weakness since childhood, aggravated by a life-time of heavy
smoking. Moreover, he was mentally exhausted. Unable to cope with the pressures of